Just Manage It!
- The 'PEOPLE' Factor

Leading and Managing
The People Around You

Colm McCormack

Preface
And Some
Words of Wisdom

"Just Manage It" is a phrase I've found myself throwing out to people over the years. Even when it comes to leading people, manage how you lead. Yes, yes…there are differences between leading and managing, but we'll cross all the semantics as we come to them. The following snippets of 'wisdom' come from this and the previous book in the *Just Manage It!* series.[1]

In business and management, simplicity and genius walk hand-in-hand.

Laziness *never* pays: it *always* costs!

So much of the quality of your life and career is heavily dependent upon the quality of the people around you and the quality of the questions you are willing to ask; most questions asked should also be asked of oneself.

---

[1] For more information on book one of the series, visit: www.JustManageIt.com

Everything is a Choice. All Choices impact upon the Demands made of you and the Constraints under which you must operate: poor choices dis-empower you.

Over time, *All* Blame Migrates.

It's not about leaving your ego at the door: you must *never* proceed beyond the door without sufficient *ego-strength*!

It is not how smart or how rich you are but how you use such things that matters; *Propensity* is the true governing factor when considering power and ability.

To be effective leading, first be prepared to follow.

Leading, managing, and example-setting are multi-directional – you can lead, manage, and bully upward too!

Management principles generally have a dark side: application is one half – defense the other.

Collaboration and Mutual-Interdependence see a slow start but a later sling-shot benefit.

A failure to move from co-acting to *inter*-acting sees us losing valuable synergies: in the silos we now have islands. It is the *Negative* Synergies we must be on guard against.

Failing to ensure that a rising tide of knowledge lifts all boats will see isolated individuals becoming unnecessarily powerful to the ultimate detriment of those around them.

The real world will often cast the optimal approach as 2nd, 3rd, or lower, on your feasibility list.

Business schools do not teach us how to manage.

The business and management worlds have been hijacked by a misplaced over-emphasis on 'Leader' as a distinct and separate person: leader*ship* yes; lead*er*, no!

There is no one-fits-all model for effective leadership or management.

It is in the understanding of people and behavior that true leadership and managerial effectiveness is to be found.

Leading and managing people is about value. The trick is not to expect people to be extraordinary: it's about getting ordinary people to perform in an extraordinary way.

Observation is the first step: experimentation and measurement should follow.

Initial focus is often best lifted from the poor performer to the Successful Deviant.

Too many "Reasons" – upon closer examination – are merely "Excuses", and pathetic ones at that.

Personnel files can be some of the most dangerous and misleading files around: Beware!

Most impactors are invisible yet still subject to management.

In business, appearance is both everything and nothing.

Conventional wisdom is not necessarily truth: even if the world believes and acts to the contrary. It is in the *creation* of and management of conventional wisdom that many people reveal themselves.

Influence is your true test of ability – *not* power.

Before managing others you should know how to manage yourself. Very often, a manager's biggest obstacle is himself. Most of us spend time tackling the by-products of our own perspectives, attitudes, and behavior.

Employees are *always* motivated and *always* creative. That they are not motivated to do what you want them to or that they exercise their creativity outside of the work setting is both your challenge and your potential failure as a manager.

People should work *with* organizations, not for them.

Jobs are very unnatural and anti-human; most people like to work but hate the confinement of a job.

Knowing the meaning of words is useless if you do not know the meaning people around you ascribe to such words.

Bureaucracy is not evil; Confrontation is necessary; Conflict can be good; knowledge of organizational politics is essential.

Everything stands or falls on communication.

The price of any stock is not always the sum total of knowledge concerning that stock: prices are often totally dependent upon the irrational forces of EMOTION.

Contents

Introduction

Most of what we will cover in this book applies whether you hold a position within the organizational managerial ranks or not. These are lessons for life – lessons you can apply for all time throughout your career.

Your **Failure Drags Others Down Too!**

I've run about five miles in temperatures touching the upper eighties. I don't have much energy left. Suddenly I become aware of a woman yelling off to my left somewhere. And there she is – a slob of a woman sitting on her front porch (yes, in emergency situations we humans make convenient stereotype-judgments). She's shouting at her kids out in the street; they're paying her *zero* attention. Then I see the reason for all the commotion: she's trying to get the kids to stop her large dog that is now charging at full speed across the front lawns of all the houses toward *me*: She can't stand or move, her kids have no respect, the dog is totally untrained. And only one thought flashes across my mind: I'm about to become the victim of a triple failure – she can't manage *herself*, she can't manage her *kids*, and she can't manage her damn *dog*! PEOPLE – you just gotta love 'em!

Education Pointed in the Wrong Direction

Business schools don't teach students how to manage people. They teach them to manage *things* – metrics, product roll-outs; to analyze, interpret, to question - but why do they fail to teach their students how to read *people*, how to analyze *people*, how to interpret *people*, how to question *people*, how to manage *people*, how to lead *people*?

Indeed, the very things business school teaches – administration, planning, strategy – are precisely the things that antagonize people and lead to fear, resistance to change, hostility, deadlock - and more.   In effect, business and management schools have been doing half the job for years.

As if seeming to compound this problem, Gallup released key findings in 2014[2] that indicate only 10% of people possess the necessary traits to be viewed as 'great managers;' not only are we in danger of teaching the wrong things to students – we may be teaching the wrong students!

Behavior

From the moment a baby is born, *everything* parents do or don't do goes toward conditioning: behavior is the main byproduct of conditioning. And the same goes for children, pets, workers.

The behavior of your executives, managers, and employees is largely the result of conditioning via your managerial philosophy, organizational culture, example setting – all underpinned by an incentive system and reward structures, tailored metrics and measures to lock in and sustain the desired behaviors. *Your* Behavior - accepted norms – conditions *them* to behave in particular ways: Blame (or praise) therefore migrates

---

[2] *Why Good Managers are So Rare*: Randall Beck and James Harter; March 13, 2014. HBR Blog Network.

back to you – or whoever is running the place - for the final results.

And yet, week-in and week-out, I encounter managers and company owners who fail to see this. I see children led from bookstores or candy aisles screaming and yelling and crying their heads off. Inconsistent management and inconsistent parenting are more abundant than we realize. As I have and will continue to say time and time again: schools don't teach you how to be a parent, pet stores don't teach you how to be a pet owner, and business schools don't teach you how to be a manager. But the commonality across all these examples is YOU: if you can manage yourself you can manage others – behavior begets behavior: accepted norms condition to create behavior in line with those accepted norms – especially when supported by suitable rewards and focused metrics![3]

Often as managers we rush out to beat workers over the heads for doing the wrong things. As you will see, one of our golden rules shall be this: *Always* start with YOU! Might your incentive system be to blame? Might your targets or goals be to blame? Let us be very clear on this point: leading and managing people effectively comes down to: (1) setting them a suitable example; (2) incentivizing them to mimic that example; (3) installing metrics to lock-in that behavior. For example; you are attentive to them, they mimic by being attentive to you and the customer, and the organization measures customer satisfaction.

There is no need to make it any more complicated than that. You are not out to change people or their personalities. A

---

[3] In very simple terms, principles of how we learn can often be viewed as follows: Operant Conditioning (reinforcement and punishment), Classical Conditioning (learning through association), and Observational Learning (Monkey see, monkey do). Rather than favor one over the other, it may well be prudent to accept a mix of all three. It is also to be recognized that not all psychologists would agree with the "From the moment a baby is born" view as expressed in the above section. That is not to say such a statement is incorrect but merely to acknowledge different schools of thought on the subject.

grumpy person can be polite or attentive or answer a telephone by the second ring – that's simply *behavior* motivated by incentives and tracked by metrics; no big mystery!

You, as manager, through the things you say and do, through your own behavior,[4] and through the systems, rules, and targets you install or preside over, are a *huge* determining factor in how the very people you are trying to manage behave. If you fail to spend time unearthing the root causes of any given behavior then you are condemning yourself to a life of managerial hardship.

Remember, organizations don't stay the same; they don't stagnate or regress or improve – organizations never change! Change is behavior; behavior is human! Change is human; status quo is human; improving, getting worse – it's all behavior; all human – think: *People*!

Experts Missing the Point Entirely

Growth, stretch targets, achieving more, greater motivation, let people set their own targets and manage themselves... We've heard this stuff so often yet it glosses over a fundamental truth. What most business books, case studies, and management gurus *don't* tell you is that there are armies of workers out there who just don't care!

Lots of people come to work for the pay check without the extra hassle. Many come to socialize, have fun. Many come because they enjoy the work they do. And many come because they *have* to.

I worked with a woman once who was the perfect and blatantly obvious choice for promotion to a new vacancy that opened up, but she didn't even put her name in the hat. As she

---

[4] See book 1 in this series for detailed discussion on example setting: *If You Cannot Manage Yourself, You Cannot Manage Others* - McCormack (2008); chapter 9.

14

later told me, she didn't want the extra hassle and stress. She simply wanted to come to work, chat with her pals, and get her work done – period.

On one occasion, I was faced with the answer, "I have a lot of family in the area", by someone refusing to seek a promotion that would easily have boosted that person's salary by 50%, if not more. The thoughts of moving a mere fifty miles down the road was a stronger *dis*incentive than a 50% pay raise was an *in*centive. Go figure!

Many "experts" out there are calling for employees to set and manage their own targets. They seem to conveniently overlook the reality on the ground: next to nobody is trained and – more importantly – *developed* to do this. It takes exceptional managers with great time and patience, a forgiving context, employees with the right attitude and desire and motivation, and more. In truth, all this "perfect management" is happening in tiny niches in miniscule ways.

Leadership or Management?

K.I.S.S. stands for: Keep It Simple, Stupid – a great rule to keep in mind. Management is often very left-brain structured; we keep things running according to a plan, to processes and systems. Leadership, on the other hand, is more right-brained creative.

Think about this. Leadership is often the name we give to acts of intervening to improve or change things; a person stepped in and got the organization moving in the right direction. Then, that new direction is formalized from its right-brained creative origins to a new left-brained management system to lock it in.

Leadership often comes first – when an organization is first put together – and then management comes second. Throughout the life of an organization, we might then expect leadership interventions to ensure ongoing constant improvement and correction.

Can one person perform both roles? Of course!! Leading and managing are verbs, not people. Don't focus on lead*er* – a distinct and separate person of supposed super human ability. Instead, focus on lead*ing*. To help you here, I will do my best throughout this book to never refer to any person as a 'Leader'; instead, I will simply mention the behavior of lead*ing* or the act of leader*ship*.

Your Personalized Leadership Brand

Whether you hold any title or rank in an organization or not, let me ask you this: If you were to think about your leadership style, could you describe your specific leadership 'brand'?

This goes to more than your identity or style; this is the every-time-guaranteed experience of and with you. Make sense? Just like any other brand, people need to know what differentiates you from the pack; they need a clear sense of who you serve; a clear sense of your guaranteed minimum standards and a consistent sense of the value you offer them and the organization through this specific, personalized leadership brand.

Damage this sense of brand – dilute it in any way – and you destroy the trust underpinning it and remove your ability to lead effectively. Guard it jealously and defend it always – especially from your own laziness or carelessness.

It is for you now to decide just what level of branding you want to apply to your leadership role: generic commodity… or something better?

Conventional Wisdom

My motto is a simple one: Conventional Wisdom is not *necessarily* truth. Far too many managers out there do things because everyone else is doing them – a sort of perverted social proof, if you will. And you'll often hear a manager say something like, "Okay, can we all come together and get some consensus on this". Wrong! Not *consensus*: FACTS![5]

Take a look at the conventional wisdom that surfaced in the early years of the twenty-first century: You *must* offer free internet or Wi-Fi to attract customers in brick-and-mortar retail outlets. Okay, let's say you run a café or something along similar lines. Your average transaction is five dollars per person. They sit for about a half-hour and then leave. So you turn each table twice per hour and generate ten dollars per table. But now you introduce free internet. Your average transaction of five dollars stays the same but people stay longer because they're surfing the web, doing college assignments, or whatever. Now they stay for three hours. Conventional *Wisdom* now sees you turning your tables once in any three hour period rather than six times, and earning five dollars in three hours instead of thirty. In this case, is conventional wisdom truth? Even if each three-hour-long visitor purchased again, they'd only be spending $10 in three hours thereby setting your table revenue generation at slightly above $3/hr – still far short of your previous $10/hr before introducing free internet.

As you will see in this book, my approach is a simple and effective one: lead, manage, and engage by walking around, ask intelligent questions, measure what you're seeing and hearing, and determine whether or not the conventional wisdom you are operating under is indeed truth or fiction. And if you cannot

---

[5] For more on this, see book 1 in this series: *If You Cannot Manage Yourself, You Cannot Manage Others* - McCormack (2008) chapter 8: *Running with the Majority*.

measure a specific thing, you can certainly measure the effects of that thing!

Always Focus on Reality

Any business or management book worth its salt *must* encapsulate and allow for the following key criteria:

- Practical experience; plus
- Academic insights; plus
- Research and evidence-based contributions; plus
- The unforeseen arrival of opportunity; plus
- The occurrence of sheer dumb luck; plus
- The unforeseen, the unexpected, and the mindboggling!

In other words, business and management books should be about the *real* world. As a manager, don't kid yourself: so much of your success is built upon help from others and a dose of unexpected circumstance with a little bit of luck and freaky timing thrown in. That is why in book one I kept repeating that everything we do as managers must be underpinned by an ability to Constantly Reassess[6] since plans, perspectives, attitudes, and circumstances are all Context Sensitive.[7] Business schools run the risk of making us slaves to models and prisoners of convenient frameworks. The human mind is geared toward taking shortcuts in order to make sense of the world around it. But there is a very fine line between shorthand and laziness. One of my key mottoes is this: in the long-run, laziness *never* pays: it *always* costs.

---

[6] See: *If You Cannot Manage Yourself, You Cannot Manage Others* - McCormack (2008); chapter 2.
[7] For discussion on the importance of Context and the need to create "Context Intelligent" managers, see book 1 of this series: McCormack (2008) chapter 7.

The Danger of Allowing the Numbers to Drive the Business

Numbers are both the aspiration and the results but must never be the sole drivers to the exclusion of all else. To allow them to take charge leads – as we have seen time and time again – to bizarre and often illegal behavior. At best, it leads to self-serving behaviors as people seek to maximize their own bonuses and managers seek to fudge the numbers before reporting to HQ. It also leads many customer service oriented companies to....well....stop serving their customers! How many retailers that pride themselves on excellent customer service cut back on employees during hard times – times when – according to their very own philosophies – they need to serve the customer more and better than ever before?!

The dollars are the result – the result of your ability to *lead and manage people* into getting behind you and following strategies that play, shape, or create the things that drive your particular industry.

Metrics

There will be dozens upon dozens of these in any organization, but here's the rub: you really do not require more than FIVE key metrics for any one point of focus!

If you launch a new marketing campaign or hiring drive or I.T. project – whatever – no more than five key metrics are required to let you know whether or not you are on target.

Oh sure, there will be sub-metrics and mountains of data; keep it simple, stupid – use the Pareto 80/20 principle: stick to no more than five key metrics at the overview level and you'll have a very fast way of knowing what is and what is not working.

My Definition for "Organizations"

Organizations are social entities, comprised of networks of people - linking to and spawning further social networks - driven by emotion and social forces.

My definition for organizations is not the standard one. So let's take a closer look at what I'm saying here.

Humans are social creatures; they are driven by emotion and social forces. You only have to look at how stocks are traded, how people react to the mainstream media, how trade unions operate, or how a rumor can rampage around an office block or warehouse, to know that fear, anger, resentment, social proof, sense of loss, conformity, fear of isolation, a desire to belong - all govern peoples' actions. Or put another way: people are often *re*actionary and *ir*rational.

The human network aspect of my definition is also key. Just watch how your fellow employees interact, work, and socialize together. Before long, you'll spot the bonds, the invisible roads they all use. Many networks pop up in every organization. These networks can transcend rank, functional silo, and gender.

Always have the network, the group, or the team in mind when dealing with an individual. Managing a person with only that person in mind is the road to ruin. They have an impact on, and are themselves impacted by, the people around them: social networks, social forces, emotions - and more.

Recurring Topics

One; *The Psychological Contract*: this is the unwritten understanding between an individual employee (of any rank) and the organization they work for. The simplest example being: if I work hard I will be rewarded for my efforts.

Two; *All Blame Migrates*: This comes from the first book in this series. In simple terms, when you are aware of something occurring and that something is someone else's fault, after a while, because you know about it, the blame for the effect actually migrates to you! Think of it this way: I'm an idiot and I cause a flood; you see the flood coming toward your house but, instead of closing the front door to avoid damage, you stand there yelling, "It's all his fault!!" Yes, you get it: because you knew and did nothing, blame migrates to you even though the original problem was caused by me. Get used to this concept popping up a lot in the organizational setting!

Three; *Constantly Reassess*: Yet again, book one in this series comes to our rescue. There, I described the need for a manager to be aware of the context in which she finds herself standing; we must see the behavior of others in context. Never take anything as a static given – constantly reassess.

Some Final Thoughts

There are three key rules in this chapter that merit repeating:

- Never forget that conventional wisdom is not necessarily truth;
- In the long-term, laziness *never* pays – it *always* costs;
- Always start with YOU – particularly the idea of your own personal Leadership Brand.

Remember that organizations are simply social entities, full of people operating via networks, underpinned by behavior and at the mercy of emotion. When dealing with any individual employee – executive, manager, or worker – you ignore the network and group implications at your peril.

Leading and managing people can often seem bothersome. But the irony of truly effective people management is that, over the long-term, you move toward managing people *less* and *away* from managing them more. So that initial "bothersome" feeling is far outweighed by the resulting benefits if you would simply frontload your efforts; put some leadership energy in upfront and everything else becomes so much easier later.

Leading and managing people in an effective way comes down to three main headings: (1) leading them through suitable example-setting; (2) rewarding the mimicking of that example-setting through incentives/remuneration; (3) supporting those incentives with suitable numbers or metrics to track, monitor, and motivate.

These key elements, over time, create the accepted norms of behavior wherein people grow through shared learning experiences – organizational culture via effective leadership and suitable managerial practices. Be aware, however; in many organizations, these three key elements – lead, incentivize, motivate - are set in opposition to one another: we have people in teams yet we review their performance on an individual basis while paying each team member different amounts of money for the same work and demanding they also cover the work of their colleagues but we punish them for not meeting their own individual numbers despite being in teams; we set examples by talking this and talking that, but then we fail to realize the metrics are demanding different things thereby causing the talked about behavior to appear delusional when compared to the actual behavior on the ground. Phew; ineffective management is exhausting!!

Chapter 1
Key Managerial Insights

Why Managers Derail

Research[8] shows that managers derail for the following key reasons:

- An absence of emotional stability;
- Defensiveness;
- Poor interpersonal skills;
- External locus of control;
- Context ignorance;
- Unsuitable example setting.

These are all things you will have to work on in yourself. In other words, before managing others you *must* learn to manage yourself: Always start with YOU!

Always Start With YOU

Whenever you encounter a problem or issue, start with yourself. This takes us back to the theory of Demands,

---

[8] We saw this in book one of this series: *If You Cannot Manage Yourself, You Cannot Manage Others* - McCormack (2008). Visit: www.JustManageIt.com for more details.

Constraints, and Choices.[9] Make the right Choice to start with yourself thereby lessening the Demands made of you and the Constraints under which you must meet those demands. Remember, most of what stands in your own way usually emanates from yourself, not from other people!

> Human nature seems to endow people with the ability to size up everybody in the world but themselves.[10]

Always check in with yourself first: you cannot truly hear what other people are saying if there is too much noise or too many emotions racing around inside your own head. Then, ask yourself some key questions:

- What evidence am I seeing (is there any??) for what I am told is happening and why it is happening?
- Have I looked to see if it is the people or the system that is causing this?
- How are my own emotions and the emotions of other people playing out and impacting the situation?
- Have I walked the floor to see and listen for myself or am I simply listening to my direct reports?
- Am I fully aware of the context in which I am standing – is this important or urgent or both?
- What are the key behaviors I am seeing? What should they be, and how were the ones I see now created or incentivized to come into being? Are we rewarding or incentivizing bad or unsuitable behaviors?

A failure to stop and ask, to go and see for yourself, to listen, to go find out, is simply a Choice that will increase the

---

[9] This theory is credited to Professor Rosemary Stewart at Oxford University. For further details, see book 1 in this series: McCormack (2008): Introduction.
[10] Maxwell (2004) p. 19.

Demands made of you and increase the Constraints under which you operate; the typical managerial response of seeking a short-term solution *devoid* of long-term focus. Remember, the demands made of you as a manager do not just relate to your job description and the task at hand. Demands also include emotional demands made by angry or worried employees, idiotic non-work related concerns, and more. You can nip a lot of these in the bud simply by starting with yourself: have *you* done enough to investigate the situation? Might *you* have caused it, even if only accidentally or unwittingly?

Your Three Key Groups

There are three key groups I recommend you form around yourself to enhance your potential for success: (1) Advisors; (2) Personal Network; (3) Chill-out Group.

First: the Advisors. This is self-explanatory. Never forget that your job is not to be the expert in all things: you are there to lead and manage the experts around you to ensure the entire organization creates and delivers high value outcomes.

Second: your Personal Network. This is a network external to your job; a network loyal to you personally that never becomes entangled in the in-house politics of the organization. Here, you may think of personal mentors, business network organizations and old experienced former colleagues or family members. No matter what occurs, these people - not being attached in any way to your organization - will always give you advice to help you personally and remain loyal to you, always you, and only you.

Third: the Chill-out Group. This is your "Head Space" time – your escape where you recharge. These are those special, sometimes quirky friends that make you laugh; they talk about off-topic things and do activities with you that refresh or rejuvenate you or help you forget yourself and the organizational stresses for a while. Remember, having key networks or groups around you is not just geared toward helping you make deals or kick ass on the business front. It's also all about being able to detox; to blow off steam; laugh about your mistakes or some occurrence in safety away from the usual prying eyes. External networks or groups also enable you hear about non-organization related things and, occasionally, act as an early warning device on topics your organization might be blind to.

Getting up close with employees can see you encounter a lot of negativity and other things that can weigh you down pretty quickly. You'll encounter a lot of problems, bitching, moaning – all draining and exhausting at first. This is why it is crucial you have an escape: a group of people unconnected with your job or workplace who are fun, easygoing, and who will pick you up or snap you out of a funk when necessary. This might seem like a trivial point now, but trust me: no escape means *precisely* that!

Shuffle the Deck

Don't kid yourself: you can't get anything done alone in life. Other people do assist you, advise you, or guide you - whether you choose to recognize this or not. But it is not the same people who always help you. Rotate faces in and out of your portfolio of advisors. As life changes, as business progresses, as you move up the ladder and/or onto new challenges, new advisors and helpers are required to answer the changing context in which you stand: new situations demand advice from different people.

It is when you use the same people all the time in every situation that you fail. It is up to you to manage the experts and people you surround yourself with and interact with.

There are two interesting points to bear in mind here: (1) a CEO, on average, changes out or reshuffles his senior team three times during the length of his tenure; (2) people who remain in the top positions for more than ten or fifteen years can scupper the dreams of an entire generation beneath them in the organization! Shuffle your team to keep both the team and yourself fresh and relevant.

The Five Most Powerful Words in Business

First, "Ask". This opens doors and saves time and effort. It lets you listen to the language people use. It enables you to empathize with them. In other words, asking them and then listening enables you to arm yourself: just turn what you're hearing back around and use it on them. Asking is also important because people like to make their own decisions – they listen to themselves when in doubt and not to someone trying to convince or change them. Anytime I come across a person who wants to start their own business I tell them to spend one hour each with five people who have been successful in what they want to go out and do: ask. Doing so can often be of greater benefit than doing an MBA and reading a library full of books.

Second, "No". This closes doors and saves time and effort. Too many of us are afraid to say no out of fear it will offend others, make us less popular, get us into trouble. "No" is a great time management technique. It's also a great weapon against those who can't manage their own workloads and who insist on getting others to do their work for them. There quite simply is not enough time in the day to get everything done. "No" helps you with this.

Third, "Because". As you will come to see in management, "because" destroys barriers and brings people along. It gives grounding to reasons and can move people from an emotional to a logical way of thinking.

Fourth, "But." In so many ways, this is the opposite of "because" – it has the potential to scupper everything: It erects barriers and puts people on the defensive. Remember, defensiveness is a key reason many managers derail. So why encourage people to fail? In other words, manage *your* words and you manage *their* behavior and success rates.

Fifth, "How". This word can open so many doors *if* used correctly and used in the right frame of mind. Instead of sitting and sulking about why you can't do something, why things aren't fair, how the economy or the markets are crap, instead ask "How?" This gets people thinking. "How" can spark creative right-brained thinking if managed correctly.

More Words and the Managerial Mindset

Words and our understanding of them can shape our perspectives, our attitudes, and – ultimately – our behavior.

"Failure" does not mean beaten. Failure is a part of managerial and business life. When you fail, pick yourself up, learn the lessons the failure is waving at you, and get going again. Sulk for a while if you must, but get going again, and soon.

Problem can mean opportunity. As Donald Trump has stated:

> I know people who see a problem as a game to be won, and they focus on solving it. I know other people who see every problem as a burden, and they are defeated before they start.[11]

---

[11] Trump (2007) p. 236.

Intelligence is not the same as attitude: your "I can" is often more important than your I.Q. Someone with the right attitude is better to have than a genius with the wrong attitude.

We've already looked at "but." We can lessen its impact with "and" and "because". This is important. Remember, as a manager you don't want to make your own job any harder than it already is: you don't want to end up managing the fallout of your own clumsiness. Saying, "I liked your presentation, but..." The "but" alerts the listener that bad news or criticism is coming thereby causing them to ignore everything that comes before the "but" and to focus instead, in a negative and defensive way, on everything coming *after* it. Instead, try something like, "I liked your presentation [because] it cut straight to the heart of the matter [because] of how you cleverly built your arguments [and] I think you can make it even better by..."[12]

"Could" is not, nor does it mean, "should". Many people despise being told what to do. They like to be the masters of their own minds and make their own decisions. Often, we hear managers tell their employees, "You should add stats to your presentation to make a greater impact". Imagine how different and more positive the reception if you said, "...*and* you *could* use stats to make an even better impression." You're getting exactly the same effect – telling the person to do a particular thing – but with a much improved response from that person.

"Opinion" is not fact – so easy to forget when confronted by other people. Be aware of who is giving you their opinion, their motivation, etc. If you have done your homework and remain confident you are onto a good thing, then take the opinions for what they are and keep moving.

If opinion is not fact, then it's not too great a leap to see that criticism is simply opinion and therefore not fact either. Not

---

[12] Don't use "however" thinking you've beaten the "but" trap. People know that "but" and "however" and "yet" and "although" can all mean the same thing!

only will you encounter failure along the way, criticism will be *everywhere* too. Obviously, you want to get as much *constructive* criticism as is helpful, but again, that too is merely opinion.

Criticism is, and is not, counsel: it depends on the motivation of the criticizer and the type of criticism given. Constructive criticism, if offered honestly and from the heart, is usually counsel: the person genuinely wants to help you. But remember: a person's own limitations, fears or outlook can cause them to offer genuine counsel that actually holds you back or damages you: them telling you that you can't do something sometimes means *they* can't do it! This is why as you progress you rotate people in and out of your advisory network. The people you seek advice from must have a mentality for the level you aspire to reach. You wouldn't talk to your local bank manager about a $100 million deal: he'd be too scared or too inexperienced to offer much worthwhile counsel.

Do you have a "Job" or do you have a "Career"? Too often I hear people foregoing happy life events or adventures because "I want to work on my career." What far too many of these people *really* mean – whether they admit it to themselves or not - is that they're going to work like a slave for years and then *maybe* they'll get recognized, and *maybe* they'll be rewarded for all their hard work, and *maybe* a promotion will come up, and *maybe*…That's a "job" baby, *not* a "career"!

"Appreciation" and "Flattery" are two different things. Watch out for the latter. This is why I want you to focus on your people skills. It's why I spent all of book 1 telling you of the need to observe people. As a manager, you need to be "people smart".

"Worrying" is not "Thinking". "Concern" is not "Worry". Dwelling upon something is not reflecting upon it. Analysis is not imagination. Pressure is not stress. Intangible does not mean inconsequential. Confronting someone does not mean conflict.

Ultimately, the words you choose as the lens through which you view and describe life, and the meanings you yourself assign to such words determines your outlook and your ability to cope and progress. It's as simple as that. Unless you can reframe many of the words you carry around in your head, you will not be as good a manager as you can be: the words you use and hear from others will simply get in your way.

You will also need to gauge the interpretation others around you have of these words to avoid creating deadlock, confusion, and unnecessary resistance and conflict. If you don't spend time considering the meaning people assign to particular words you simply make life more difficult for yourself.

Generalist versus Specialist

> Specialization, for all its benefits, tends to limit the sort of cross-boundary learning that generates breakthrough ideas. It can also lead to parochialism and venomous turf battles. If not checked, the quest for ever greater standardization can metastasize into an unhealthy affection for conformance, where the new and the wacky are seen as dangerous deviations from standard operating procedures.[13]

There will always be a place for the Specialist, but it is the elevation of the Specialist to the position of be-all and end-all by society, the business schools and the business world, that we need to guard against.[14]

A Specialist in a specialist's functional setup will of course be successful. But put him to the top as CEO and ask him to skillfully and deftly manage all specialist functions in harmony devoid of silo-type mentality while at the same time maximizing

---

[13] Hamel (2007) p. 152.

[14] It has often been quipped that becoming a specialist involves learning more and more about less and less.

human synergies to the combined benefit of all and he will not be as successful as the Generalist.

Focus more on "Leader*ship*", NOT "Lead*er*"

I have nothing against the concept of leadership, but the focus on *leader, leader, leader,* is something that bothers me. Overuse of the term "leader" in today's business world has become a convenient form of escape and denial. We are told that a leader sets the vision for us, gets us to move toward it, inspires us along the way and generates trust, commitment, and buy-in. But the actual truth is that such a person creates and then manages the vision, your perception of it, and their own behavior – it's all leadership and management with a "leader" sticker on it thereby giving the impression of a different person – an almost super being - a chosen one, if you will.[15]

Leader obsession by the business world contributes not just to general disillusion, but also to spiraling pay disparities, rising CEO costs[16] and general unhappiness in the ranks.

Good Enough[17]

Anyone who has ever set up a business from scratch will know exactly what I'm talking about here: just make it *good enough*.

You don't have time to sit around waiting for perfection. Things *do* change. You *will* overlook certain things but you *will* adapt along the way. Remember what I said all business and management books should allow for – facts, research, but also

---

[15] For more detailed discussion, see book 1 in this series: *If You Cannot Manage Yourself, You Cannot Manage Others* - McCormack (2008) chapter 10.
[16] See: Pfeffer (2007) chapter 27.
[17] An approach highlighted strongly by Carayol et al, (2001).

the unforeseen, sheer dumb luck. The point is to get going in the first place. Get everything into an okay shape and get moving. So long as it's good enough, hit the road; perfection is a journey, *not* a point from which to start!

Call for a Time Out

It has often been argued that a happening only becomes an experience *after* you reflect on that experience. Certainly it only becomes a worthwhile learning experience if you take time out to look back on what led up to it, what occurred, and what it should mean going forward.

Reflection is not just a development tool for managers: it is a development tool for *all* humans irrespective of their occupation, position, or title. As I stated in book one[18], living *is* managing. If you find yourself emerging from chaos in the mornings - going to work - and then returning home to chaos, then you are doing something wrong. Management and leadership principles are not just for work; they apply to life too. So reflecting on the events that occur in the work setting is not enough: doing so benefits your personal/family life too.

Never be afraid to walk away from a situation. One of the keys to effective decision-making is in knowing how much time you have to make the decision. Be aware of people who – deliberately or unwittingly – create in you a false sense of urgency or lack of time.

It is important that you sneak away for a little "head space" everyday. I solve most of my problems in the shower! It's probably because at that hour of the morning my brain has not yet been overloaded by a full day's events. It's also because a lot of things get solved by the human mind when it is somewhere between serious work and leisure: a little lull or taking the foot

---

[18] McCormack (2008).

off the gas for a bit seems to jump us onto the right track. As one of my old professors - Professor Kingston – from Trinity College states:

> …revolutionary ideas are born in leisure and freedom from external pressures, away from work, by not being too absorbed in the completion of day-to-day tasks. Leisure, freedom of spirit, being 'distanced' in some way from the source of major pre-occupations, is a key element in all creative work… *The source of new ideas is the unconscious mind, tilled by conscious labour.* It is to allow time for this 'tilling' to take effect that some people advocate attacking problems on a two-stage basis, with time between for the ideas of the first stage to germinate, as it were, as a result of deliberate inaction. As Renoir put it, 'you must know how to loaf a bit' – and his output as a painter shows that this has nothing to do with laziness.[19]

Go stare at the traffic for a while or whatever it takes. As kids we were told not to daydream, to wake up. Nonsense! Daydreaming is the body's natural relaxation technique: it's soothing, comforting, and good. So daydream a little. So long as you don't do it while operating dangerous machinery, you'll be fine. Just make sure you get that valuable headspace time. Many problems are solved by not thinking about them. Just like when you're trying to remember the name of a book or person, it's on the tip of your tongue, but just won't come to you. So what do you do? That's right: you *stop* thinking about it and then it comes back to you. The same with management: a little time-out enables you sling-shot ahead later.

Start Working SMART!

If all you do is manage the functions – Marketing, HR, Finance, Sales – and rant and rave to get people to meet their metrics, you're not working smart.

They don't tell you in business school that a huge part of your job should be teaching. By teaching and developing those

---

[19] Kingston (2003) p. 199-200.

around you, you make your own job easier. You can create the leaders of tomorrow thereby adding value to the organization as a whole, enhancing the succession strategy and giving the company the option of promoting from within.

Teaching and developing will see you moving away from the dead end "control" managerial mindset toward one of "influence" – you move from left-brain management to right-brained leadership (again, without becoming a totally different form of being!) When you help people you reinvigorate the psychological contract.[20] In time, you become an "employer of choice" as word spreads throughout the industry from satisfied employees that you are a good manager or employer.

As with all the warm-and-fuzzy aspects of leadership, your job is not to waste huge swaths of time teaching while the business of the organization goes down the toilet. As we saw in my earlier book – *The YOU Factor: If You Cannot Manage Yourself, You Cannot Manage Others* – all concepts are Context Specific.

On the teaching and development front, these are simply things you make part of your everyday work activities – no big deal.

Your Decision Making

The longer you put them off, the more you procrastinate, the more you worry, stress, and then search for more and more information. But when you make the decision, you instantly feel better. That's because you now have a sense of direction. Be informed, but avoid paralysis-by-analysis. Remember, *good enough*!

---

[20] A psychological contract is a non-spoken agreement between an employee and his/her employer e.g. if I work hard I'll be rewarded. In book 1 we discussed the dangers of *Warping the Psychological Contract*. See: *If You Cannot Manage Yourself, You Cannot Manage Others* - McCormack (2008) chapter 8.

You won't get it right all the time but you *will* improve your success rate as you go. You will have to learn to assess all the information available, make the decision, and then get going on all the other things awaiting your attention.

First, know how much time you have available to make the decision – don't be pressured needlessly;

Second, keep in mind the direction the organization or project needs to move in - don't get distracted by the bright shiny pennies along the way;

Third, move from a decision-making mindset of *right-versus-wrong* to one of *different-plus-better*. Sometimes you need to take smaller steps and a longer way around to reach your destination – cultivate a sense of patience while remaining flexibly focused.

If it turns out, despite all the care in the world, you still make the wrong call, simply decide to fix it, and then fix it: good enough!

Some Final Thoughts

Remember those five important words when dealing with people in business and management: (1) Ask, (2) No, (3) Because, (4) But, and (5) How. The way in which you use them and how the people around you use and interpret them determines just how successful you can become.

Don't become blinded by "Lead*er*" or feel inadequate if no one pins that label on you. Focus, instead, on exercising effective leadership.

Specialize if you must, but always lean toward becoming a generalist. Keep your options open. Understand numerous disciplines and the links between them - add value to yourself as an individual.

Keep your own personal networks of (1) advisors within the organization; (2) external advisors and mentors loyal to *you* and not the company you work for; (3) Chill-out people to enable you escape and recharge.

Teach as you go. Employees are depreciating assets – especially those at the management and executive levels. Allowing the tools that do the work to become dull makes no sense.

Always start with YOU! It's good for you, good for others, and good for the business – book one of this series dealt specifically with this topic.

Don't become obsessed with perfection. Get things into "Good Enough" shape, then hit the road improving and perfecting as you go.

Flexibility in approach and of thinking, together with unrelenting persistence, a sense of humor, and the ability to zone out for some head space – especially when things hit the fan – are key ingredients to success in business and management.[21]

---

[21] All items discussed in detail in book 1 of this series. See: McCormack (2008).

Chapter 2
Looking at Employees

Sizing up the People Around you

The New Workplace Reality

With the 21st century well and truly under way, the workplace, and the people in it, is radically different from twenty years ago. As Forbes and Deloitte point out:[22]

- 60% of employees feel overwhelmed;
- The proliferation of technology – thereby ensuring employees are 'always on' – has destroyed work-life balance;
- Employees are too distracted: they check their phones as much as 150-times per day;
- Employees are flooded with too many calls, emails, meetings;
- Average focus or attention span has dropped noticeably over the years.

Management and leadership sound like attractive propositions in the face of such a reality, don't they?! Now let's

---

[22] Why Companies Fail to Engage Today's Workforce: The Overwhelmed Employee.

move from employee behavior to employee demands of many of the best places to work:[23]

- Challenge;
- Freedom;
- Control;
- Respect;
- Success experiences;
- Positive expectations.

The working world as we know it is becoming a very 'interesting' place indeed!

Start at the Top

Get it wrong with the top team and it's all over – sooner or later. To repeat a well-used business analogy: It is crucial you get: (1) the right people; (2) on the bus; (3) sitting in the right seats; (4) doing the right things. These people must be loyal to this top team, not to their individual departments or functions or silos. They must embody the organizational culture – living it; promoting it; sustaining it.

The Danger of Personnel Files

The work of managing people very often begins *before* you start working at an organization or new post. My advice to managers is always this: Resist the temptation to open personnel files. As a new manager you must take the time to meet people face-to-face, get a feel for who they are, their attitudes, what they think has made the business successful, what they think is

---

[23] http://www.briantracy.com/blog/business-success/best-places-to-work-work-environment-business-ethics#ixzz2vqWTy7d4

holding it back, and more. It is for *you* as the manager to form *your own* assessment of peoples' capabilities, attitudes and future potential value to the business. You rarely find what you really need to know in a personnel file. And here's why:

- Personnel files were not compiled by *you*;
- The opinions and views of someone else, at that time, in that context, are all that such files contain;
- Inconsistent record keeping may have been the norm;
- Personal grudges may have motivated much of the recording;
- Bad managers picking on people may have been the *real* problem whereas the file will show the *employee* as being the problem;
- The views of others, at the time they were expressed, in the context in which they were expressed, and with the views of the past, present, and future held by those others can prejudice your mind and create bias;
- The recordings in the files may be totally wrong;
- The recordings may be 100% correct but under the organizational culture *currently* in place or in place at the time the recordings were made;
- Such files are rarely holistic in nature and catch only pieces of the overall picture;
- People can be certified in certain things (a plus) but have become driven by bad habits (negating the plus).

Personnel files can contain a lot of truth, but laziness is *not* a characteristic of the excellent manager. Set out a timetable. Never ignore warnings and bad individual histories, but do spend your first few weeks getting to know everyone around you. Then, and only then, open the personnel files and see what you think of the content.

Lead, Manage, and Engage by Walking Around

It's not the walking around that counts: it's what you're looking at, the questions you ask, and what you are listening to as you walk. The aim is *mental,* not physical exercise.

You can't get a real feel for a person unless you're standing there with them face-to-face. There is so much more to communication than simply the words spoken: facial expression, posture, body language, facial color, prolonged silence, a refusal to make eye contact – they all enable you to hear what is *not* being said.[24] Personnel files, charts, facts and figures can all dehumanize and block out a lot of the message you need to be hearing.

Be genuine, be empathetic to workers' individual subjective views, and have a positive regard for each person you are interacting with.[25] When people pick up on these key ingredients – genuineness, empathy, positive regard – a more beneficial and workable relationship becomes possible. Don't spend hours; don't waste time – simply engage with people regularly. Remember: to lead, you must first follow! This is a golden principle you should never lose sight of. Only by getting in with the people on the ground and learning from them first, can you ever hope to later lead them effectively. Your rank or title does not define you: your behavior does, so lead by doing some upfront following.

Insights into the People around You

First, view employees in the best possible light. This does not mean become a fool, turn a blind eye, or operate like an

---

[24] For more in-depth discussion on communication in business and management, see book 1 of this series: *If You Cannot Manage Yourself, You Cannot Manage Others -* McCormack (2008) chapter 6.
[25] Genuineness, Empathy, and Positive Regard are qualities expressed by Rogers in the field of humanistic psychology and client-centered psychotherapy.

idiot. Viewing employees in the best possible light brings the Pygmalion Effect into play. Simply stated, people can sense from you whether or not you hold high or low expectations of their abilities and potential for success; you unwittingly communicate your thoughts to people via your attitude, behavior, enthusiasm – or lack of all these things.[26] This *could* have an impact in the actual outcome. The most commonly quoted experiment out there is the one in which a teacher is told a handful of students have shown promise and are expected to excel. In truth, the handful – unknown to the teacher – were simply picked at random. In the end, they *did* excel and simply because the teacher *thought* they would. This effect works best with people who have never met previously.[27]

Second, knowing the factors that influence a person is of immense benefit to a manager who must deal with the behavior of that person. There are three main factors: Biological, Psychological, and Socio-Cultural. Some psychologists will view each of these as separate branches whereas others will take them all in a holistic approach. My point to you, however, is this: you cannot know anything about a person's moods, psychological makeup, or their family or social influences without engaging with them to some degree. Gaining insight into such things not only enables you to determine why certain behaviors occur: it enables you to see the best way to lead and manage the person in different contexts.

Third, the Hidden Self Diagram:[28]

---

[26] Pessimistic expectations can bring about what is known as the "Golem Effect".

[27] For more in-depth discussion on the Pygmalion Effect, see: Manzoni et al (2002).

[28] Just Manage It! *If You Cannot Manage Yourself, You Cannot Manage Others*. McCormack (2008): Introduction.

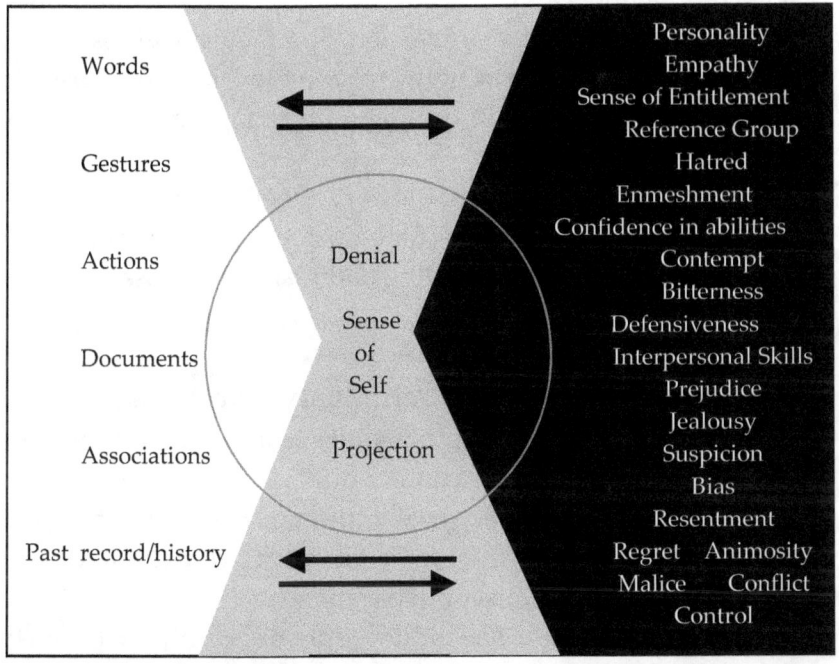

© 2008 Colm McCormack

What we see in a person's behavior is quite small. What lies in the shadows, however, can be far more important. Read the words on the left of the diagram – the ones out in the light. If you read the diagram from left to right, through the center and into the dark, things start to become interesting. Everything a person does must first run through the filter at the center of the diagram. It is for you as a manager to discover what lies in the dark in order to see why the items out in the light manifest in the way they do.[29]

Fourth, you should be aware that five key dimensions of personality have been found to be related to important work-

---

[29] For more in-depth discussion on the Hidden Self diagram, see book 1 in this series: McCormack (2008).

related tendencies.[30] Agreeableness, conscientiousness, emotional adjustment, extroversion, and inquisitiveness have all been found to be strongly related to task mastery, job performance, resilience in dealing with change, group cohesion, and solution generation.

Taking all of the points above, a better understanding of *why* people behave the way they do gives you the potential to become more effective in leading and managing those people.

Assessing Them – Some Preliminary Questions

First, start with your immediate team. If this is not as it should be, then you *will* encounter difficulties - guaranteed.

Second, make certain your top team realize their number one duty is loyalty to the senior team that you run and *not* to their individual functions or departments.

Third, make sure the right people are on the team in the right roles doing the right things.

Here are some of the *preliminary* questions you should ask yourself when assessing employees – managers *and* general employees - to get a feel for what's going on in the organization:

• Are they displaying any signs of emotional instability?
• Are there any or many outbursts – does anyone seem to have anger issues or seem unapproachable?
• Are they defensive when receiving feedback or criticism?
• Do they blame a lot? Are they failing to be accountable and take responsibility?
• Are they offering "Reasons" *or* "Excuses"? – There's an important difference!

---

[30] Vecchio (2006).

- Do they display an awareness of context or do they just keep doing the same thing and offering the same tired old solutions?
- Any signs of learned helplessness from relying too heavily on others around them?
- Do they seem surprised when you ask them to contribute or make a suggestion?
- Do they seem reluctant to answer or overly mistrustful?
- Any nervous laughs when they are challenged or feeling uneasy?
- Are any employees withdrawn from the people around them, from a particular supervisor, from their team, or from you?
- Can you trace a knowledge map from what you are observing?
- Can you trace a political map from what you are observing?
- Can you trace the key relationship flow patterns (who actually interacts with whom across functions and rank) from what you are observing?
- Are there many closed doors to peoples' offices?
- Are the blinds closed too?

You should never assume maturity develops at the same pace a person ages. This goes for both employees and managers. These questions help you unearth key behaviors that point to causes you need to start managing rather than symptoms that serve only to distract.

Remember, managers derail because of defensiveness, emotional instability and poor inter-personal skills. The questions above are aimed at looking to see if such problems exist. Occasionally, employees with 'problems' are simply working under one Big Problem: their manager!

How to Investigate: Structure Your Conversations

Uniformity and consistency – obtain value and answers from your interactions; nothing I am advocating in this book should be construed as time wasting or fluffy touchy-feely nonsense.

Ask everybody the *same* questions: it's as simple as that. Doing so enables you to rate people across the same topics, the same insights, the same outlooks. By standardizing your questions across generalized topics, you get a feel for the prevailing consensus view in the business.

You are always looking for the successful deviants: people in the business who are bucking the general trend in a positive way. Often you will find there is one store in a district that is outperforming the others. But as managers we generally start visiting the worst performing store, or unit, or restaurant, or sales division, to kick them in the pants and put their ass in line. But this is very like my rule of not opening the personnel file until you've done everything else. If you visit the problem area first, you'll prejudice your own mind and arrive with the simple bias that they're crap. If, however, you go out and get a feel for what the successful deviant in the pack is doing, you then have something to compare the poor performer against other than metrics and stats. The metrics, stats, goals, targets – they all show a result but not necessarily a reason for *why* things are the way they are.

And it's the same with people. Find out who the positive deviants in the business are – the ones doing the best – and go watch what they do and listen to what they tell you. Probe, keep digging, ask meaningful questions and then shut up and listen.

Observation: Take it Another Step

In Book One[31] I told you to spend a lot of time observing the people around you. I told you not to dive into trying to manage people but to first spend time watching and listening to them without interfering. See how they impact on the Five Constituencies: (1) People around them; (2) Themselves; (3) the Organization; (4) External Stakeholders, and (5) You. Doing so enables you to see so much more of what is *actually* going on: frontload the effort and you'll save yourself lots of time on the backend. You've been looking at the world all your life – now it's time to start *seeing* it. Management is a deeply human interactive experience; it is a human activity - so start watching humans!

Once you have a clear picture of who hangs out with whom, who really makes the decisions, who the real experts are, who the company historians are, who the grumps and unapproachables are - and more - you can then move to step 2 of the observation process: experimenting.

Remember that a lot of what you see as a manager is all surface material. That's precisely why you spend time observing and getting a feel for the people you work with. Just as soon as you think you're seeing things for what they really are, test your assumptions and conclusions. Try things out. Ask questions. Clarify. Run things by people. Make sure you're right. It doesn't take much time or extra effort just to make sure.

But let's keep things simple for now. Let's say you suspect one of your new team or employees of being the gossip monger who infects everyone else with nonsense. Test your conclusion: tell a few different people a different story each and see which story gets back to you. Experimenting *should* be *that* simple.

---

[31] McCormack (2008): *If You Cannot Manage Yourself, You Cannot Manage Others.*

Look for "Resident Rebels" and "Career Whiners"

What I term "Resident Rebels" are people who always seem to be causing trouble. You may also come across people who have spent their entire working lives complaining: "Career Whiners". I've come across lots of these people, but here's a punch line many managers don't expect: once in a while, the same people constantly complaining about the *same* small number of things actually have a point. A lot of the time it's the managers they're complaining to that are the *real* problem. Again, personnel files blind: *You're* in charge: Go find out what's *really* going on!

Do You Have Any "Brilliant Dullards"?

People interested in the dull and unadventurous seem to be the enemy to guard against according to most guru-style business and management books out there. But you quite simply cannot escape the fact that you will always require some people who are brilliant at doing the same thing and who do not want to advance any farther: what I term "Brilliant Dullards".

You will always need people who are good at doing the same thing, reinforcing it, presiding over it, and with little interest or motivation to change. Core processes and systems may require constant improvement in something as large as a Toyota manufacturing plant, but most of us simply need to install good systems and then leave Brilliant Dullards running them efficiently and effectively. In the real world, it's often *that* simple!

Do You Have Any "Cowardly Lions"?

One time, a group of PhD students were told by their university that they had to travel overseas to attend a program.

The price looked far too high but the group refused to push back. I started shouting from the sidelines and suddenly the price came down by half. Now I was *really* suspicious!

But what got to me the most was how each of these people was alarmingly cowardly in their dealings with people around them. This, in part, is because people confuse confronting a person with conflict: we saw this in Book One.[32] It's also a fear of how the other person might react. Alarmingly, however, it shows an inability to manage a situation properly, a failure to manage inter-personal issues, and all these qualities were to be found in people who would later have to manage others!

You need to know if you have any Cowardly Lions onboard. These people don't fight for price concessions from vendors, suppliers, distributors, or anybody. They cave in too easily. They're afraid to raise concerns. In the work setting they're apt to bury such concerns since going to their boss equates to a sign of weakness on their part and the danger of having to confront an issue. Salesmen love these kinds of people because they can sell lots to them at ridiculous prices.

You also need to be on the lookout for cowardly managers. You know the type – they send around general emails saying things like, "It is important that everyone arrives to work on time". We all know damn well that it's one or two certain individuals who keep arriving late yet we *all* get the email. These to-everybody-type emails or statements don't work because:

- The offender doesn't realize that they are the target of the message; or
- They *know* you're talking about them but because *you* don't have the balls to call them out on it they use your cowardice against you: they hide among the crowd, and

---

[32] McCormack (2008), Chapter 5.

- The group knows who the non-performer is and your approach:
  - o Is viewed as a criticism of everyone;
  - o Causes the group to become angry with the offender *and* with *you*, and
  - o You look like the cowardly manager you are.

Think about the logic these managers follow: instead of confronting that one person I'm going to piss *everyone* else off instead. Always remember, the good diligent workers suffer more than the average worker when slighted so cowardly managers end up warping the psychological contract against the company.[33]

Do You Have Any Passive-Aggressive People?

A passive-aggressive personality is someone who is aggressive but in a passive way. They attack from behind the scenes. Let me give you an example.

Charlie corrects Colm for a mistake he is making on the job. Two minutes after being corrected, Colm makes the same mistake again and both he and Charlie share a joke and laugh about it. But Charlie reported the laughing episode in a different way. In essence, he laughed in public but then went straight up the backstairs and whispered a warped version of what occurred into the Manager's ear: "*Colm won't do what he's told and seems to be a slow learner*".

---

[33] Warping the Psychological Contract was a major theme in book 1 of this series. It is my view that in badly run companies such contracts can be warped against the company through poor and ineffective management practices. There is ample scope to suggest that once the psychological contract has been warped against an organization, there is no such thing as a restoration of a good position. Once lost it is gone forever, so the "return" is in fact a *new* position. For more, see book 1: McCormack (2008) chapter 8.

Here are two things to bear in mind when dealing with such people: when confronted they will (1) deny, and then (2) become defensive. These people are usually insecure and do not like confrontation: that's why they're cowardly sneaks. So you'll have to manage in anticipation of such reactions. You'll be confronting an insecure person who will deny everything at first and then immediately become defensive if you keep after him.

The damage these people cause can be enormous. They destroy trust. They spread suspicion. They warp the psychological contract against the business and start to slowly convert the organizational culture into one of cloak and dagger – the nasty version of organizational politicking.

Root these people out. Limit their impact. Deal with them fast. Tell them they must deal with people openly and not allow personal animosity to drag on for weeks. Passive-aggressiveness is not a mental disorder: it's a form of behavior – a *modus operandi*. You'll save yourself a lot of hassle by developing them toward more suitable behaviors - or ditching them altogether.

Different Kinds of Trouble-Makers

What I term "Beneficial Trouble-Makers" are those who play the role of Devil's Advocate. They are change agents, thought provokers, and bring sharpness to the business. These people can be of immense value if engaged, tested, and listened to. The other type – the "Hindering Trouble-Makers" – require little if any introduction. They object to everything, won't move an inch, moan, complain – they hinder progress, improvement, dialogue, and more.

You need to go find out for yourself which type any person labeled as a trouble-maker is – Beneficial or Hindering? – otherwise you could end up taking a serious misstep.

The Wolf in Sheep's Clothing

Never assume a negative person is always someone who presents as depressed or gloomy or dismissive or terrible to be around or not open to discussing new ideas. I've encountered many very happy intelligent people who always had different yet brilliant ways of killing off all suggestions and ideas offered to them.

One day – tired of this phenomenon in a particular individual – I drew a grid on a piece of paper with the headings: *'My Suggestion'*; *'Your Answer'*; *'Actual Answer'*; *'Result'*. I entered each suggestion I made. I was amazed at the intelligence – the brilliantly insightful references to past examples – that came back to me from this guy as answers to each suggestion; but then things started to become clear as I entered results into the last two columns: his *'Your Answer'* each time was, in effect, a "No" to every suggestion; the *'Result'* from every conversation was that all things – despite clear and recognized problems - remained the same!

Are They Looking Away From the Oncoming Car?

Have you ever been driving when suddenly some guy steps out into the street just ahead of you - he sees you coming but spends his entire time crossing the street looking the other way? Drivers who pull out in front of faster moving cars often do the same thing: "If I don't look it won't hit me", seems to be their thinking.

A lot of people manage their personal finances the same way: if I don't monitor what I'm spending or don't look at my bank account for this month I'll be fine. And they do it in business too: not looking at how they're doing on their budget until after the mid-year point and other such things.

First, make sure this person is not *you*. Second, go find out if any of these people are hiding in the ranks. Denial can be a very dangerous thing. Step out into the street in Dublin or Rome with the attitude of "If I just don't look they won't hit me" and there's a good chance that eventually you *will* get hit, and hit *hard*. The same in business: turning a blind eye does not enable you to see whether or not the other guy has stepped on the gas, or if spending is getting out of control, or if competitors have suddenly moved.

Do They Make Eye-Contact?

Watch how employees and managers interact with clients, customers, and each other in face-to-face settings. Do they make eye-contact? This is absolutely crucial for generating trust, relationship building, and for putting people at ease.

I remember being on a connector flight to JFK in New York. There, staff at the desk would say, "Yes, can I help you?" without ever looking up. They'd keep typing or reading. We asked our questions and they would then reply, again without looking up. Conclusion: whether rightly or otherwise, we wanted out of that part of America ASAP! Now imagine that instead of being at an airport we were visiting your store or offices and we left with those same feelings toward your business. All because someone simply did not look up, make eye-contact, smile, and give an impression of warmth and attentiveness. Never forget: every interaction a customer or client has with your organization is a value creating or value destroying touch point.

Again, your starting place will always be with YOU. If employees have learned this from you because that is how *you* treat *them*, or if you have failed to insist they make eye-contact, then blame is migrating to you on this point.

Think of poor interaction with customers, clients, and employees as a lagging indicator: you won't feel the negative impact until it's too late!

What Impact do their Surroundings Have?

Far too often we spend our time watching people and miss a key component in shaping their behavior: their surroundings.

When looking at others, go back to the Five Constituencies. How is each person impacting on those around them and the organization as a whole? Do you see anyone who is their own worst enemy? Do you see anyone who drags those around them down, prevents positive change, rallies people to the wrong side?

You might find that the equipment your employees have is not as good as it could be. The factory or office may be laid out in such a way that people have to walk miles everyday or have places to disappear into.

We often made the mistake of separate bathrooms, canteens, and gathering areas for managers, employees, and eggheads.

> ...wherever there is an intellectual barrier between activities, it should never be reinforced by a physical barrier.[34]

Common gathering areas where people from different disciplines, different functions, and different ranking levels can congregate, chat, share stories and problems, and brain storm for solutions are all excellent examples of how surroundings can help or hurt. Remember, down with barriers, up with interaction and diversity.

Have you ever walked a factory floor and noticed how dull and depressing the place is? How cheap and easy do you think

---

[34] Kingston (2003) p. 51.

it would be to get everyone in there feeling a little better? That's right: paint the place! Show a little pride.

Small inexpensive changes can often produce disproportionately large positive effects. Might your employees' surroundings be responsible for something? How are the surroundings impacting upon their behavior – for better or worse? If you don't know – go find out!

How Are They Motivated?

Has anybody ever told you that their dog just sleeps all day long, or their kids just watch TV all day, or their workers fart around on the internet and take too many cigarette breaks? Do the people uttering these statements not realize that blame must surely be migrating toward *them* and *not* the dog, the kids, or the workers? Obviously not because I'm still hearing these things everyday.

In 2009, I wandered through the back offices of a well-known American retailing giant and noticed some of the employees watching a sales training video. In the video, the VP was telling those who were watching that if they could raise sales in their part of the store by just $6 per hour, that in turn would raise profits for the entire organization by 6% (or some such amount). As I stood eavesdropping, only one thought ran through my mind: all these people were supposed to work their butts off and who would get the benefit of all this work? That's right – the guy in the video! *His* share options would benefit. *His* numbers would look great. *His* bonus would go up. *His* basic salary would improve. But the workers? They got to *feel good*!

If you're trying to inspire people at the bottom with things like improving earnings per share and the like, you're probably an idiot. You certainly don't sound like someone who does a lot of walking around, asking the right questions, and listening to the answers. These workers don't benefit from achieving the goals you're talking about. You're not even on the same page as them.

Remember, people are *always* motivated. To get them motivated to do what you want them to do you need to understand them – and you'll understand them if you engage with them as you walk around.

How Do They Think – How Do They Process?

Only by spending time around people can you discover how they think and how they process information. Having this knowledge is key to effective management and leadership: it provides the ability to work *smart*, rather than hard.

Think about your immediate team; do you know who thinks in pictures? Who thinks in sound? Would you know who thinks emotionally or thinks in words? You'll notice some can remember files by the numbers assigned to those files; others remember by the circumstances; some by the clients' names.

Knowing how people think and process allows you to alter your communication approaches to increase your chances of effectiveness and success with them; different people need different forms of information to process and operate effectively.

Do You Have An Engagement Problem?

Disengagement – misplaced motivation[35] - is one of the real consequences of poor or ineffective management. Business school has many of us looking at the accounts. But a lot of bad things don't show up on the accounts because there is no place for them, no label, and often no way of measuring these things;

---

[35] "Misplaced" because people are *always* motivated. An engagement problem is simply an indication their motivation is placed/based outside of the work setting.

all we see are symptoms but not the cause. Or, perhaps more to the point, often there is very little Will or not enough time to measure such things.

The costs are to be found in absenteeism rates, in dropping productivity figures, in increased theft by employees, in increased accidents suffered by employees, in the increasing numbers of employees quitting and going some place else and your increased hiring and training costs that result. These are the things to measure and then set about managing. But make sure you manage the *reasons* these things are happening. Marching out to rant and rave and beat employees over the heads without tackling the cause will simply add to your problems. Don't be a lazy manager.

> It is not unusual, for example, for some retailers to endure 100 percent annual turnover. Executives in such industries often chalk up the comings, goings, and perpetual new-recruit training as an unavoidable cost of hiring low-wage, college-aged people whose lives have not stabilized. Yet within the churn lies a hidden cost of poor managing: business units with a surplus of disengaged employees suffer 31 percent more turnover than those with a critical mass of engaged associates.[36]

Are You Creating Presenteeism?

Now let's bring all of these things together – motivation, disengagement, poor and ineffective management, an inability or unwillingness to understand behavior, and incentives that bring about undesired behaviors. All of these things can create the phenomenon known as "Presenteeism": Being present and still contributing nothing!

I despise how modern textbooks simply define presenteeism in terms of people who are too ill to work yet come to work anyway thereby infecting others. I believe this should be expanded to people who surf the internet, chat on the phone

---

[36] Wagner et al (2006) p. xiv.

all day to friends and family, who take too many cigarette breaks - and more. After all, people who engage regularly in these activities to the extreme are present yet contributing nothing; such people are a cost to the business, a distraction to their colleagues and playing the role of social loafers.

But remember one of our golden rules: Always start with YOU. Might *you* be the cause of all this? Did *you* implement any of the things that cause this? If not, might *you* be reinforcing and presiding over the cause of all the problems? Remember, it's no excuse to say your predecessor put all these things in place. You're the boss *now*, so get to fixing it.

Shoot the Turkeys

Some people will simply have to go. First, you should decide whether your immediate senior team contains people who need to move on. As a CEO, you should be changing out/refreshing your senior team several times over the course of your tenure. Remember, get this team wrong and the entire organization is in trouble.

Second, move to employees in general. Some people simply will not buy into the changes you want to bring about and the direction you want to move the business in. It doesn't matter if it's your number one sales guy: if he doesn't get onboard he'll become a source of disruption and, in time, a rallying point for others. If they're not getting onboard they need to go sail on another ship.

In the end, you need to deal with the person but focus on all the other employees you'll be sandbagging if you become overly concerned about hurting the person in question. Keeping a person who needs to move on is unfair to the people who have to work with this person, unfair to you and the organization, unfair to customers and clients, and ultimately, unfair to the person himself.

Some Final Thoughts

The entire point behind this chapter was to stop you diving in to lead people you don't yet fully understand. To lead, you must first follow! What is it that creates their current behaviors? Gain insights into what makes them tick and managing them becomes so much easier: lead and manage from a position of informed intelligence.

Don't start with the personnel files. Take the time to go talk with people and listen to what they're telling you. If at first they don't open up, then keep walking around and keep talking to them. In time, after a few weeks, the nut *will* start to crack.

Walk around everyday. Interact with employees. Ask questions. Listen. Make sure you understand what you are hearing. Leading, managing, and engaging by walking around is *mental* exercise, *not* physical: it develops you *and* employees. Don't spend all day doing it or fall into paralysis-by-analysis; you have a business or department to run – no need to over-egg the pudding!

Observe, test your hunches (experiment), measure. Move away from anecdotal-type management and toward measurement and evidence-based management.

Never forget that occasionally rebels, troublemakers and complainers *may* actually have a point!

Look at the factory or offices – do they promote work and positivity or is the place a dump and dragging everyone down? Are things set up right in terms of productivity and efficiency? Can people from different levels and disciplines intermingle regularly? Do they? Can you see why or why not?

Determine whether or not anyone needs to be told to move on. If so, get it done: you're only as strong as your weakest link.

If you follow my train of thought in this chapter, you'll have:

- Met everyone in the organization;
- Listened to their ideas;
- Heard what they like and don't like;
- Listened to the reasons they believe the business has been successful;
- Listened to them telling you the few small things they believe require changing in order to make their jobs easier;
- You'll have unearthed what does or does not motivate them;
- You'll have discovered whether or not incentives are working and whether or not incentives are causing people to behave in unexpected ways;
- You'll have discovered who the cranks, the unapproachables, the whiners, and the rebels are;
- You'll have discovered who has the right attitude to move the business forward and whether or not they're sitting in the right places doing the right things;
- You'll have gained valuable insights into the personality characteristics, skills, and interpersonal skills of each person;
- You'll have found out where the knowledge is in the business, how politics is played, who the main power brokers are and who hangs out with whom.

You want to operate from a constant executive mindset that silently roars, "Get out of their way!" Hire good people, give them the tools to do what they do best, then reduce bureaucracy and politics and nonsense – the getting out of their way part – so they can do what you pay them to do. Remember: (1) lead by suitable example; (2) incentivize to promote mimicking of that example; (3) install metrics to keep the suitable behavior flowing constantly.

Chapter 3
Interact and Engage

Working on Relationships

A little selfishness can be a very healthy thing. In relationships, a small amount of it enables you to retain a sense of self and enables you avoid drifting into a life that, in the long-term, could bring you unhappiness or lack of fulfillment.

The same with the idea of getting out of employees' way: when you get out of *their* way, you get out of *your own* way! Making such a Choice lowers the Demands made of you and the Constraints under which you must operate – a better all-round relationship.

In a way, all business is relationships. There is ample scope to suggest relationships see us either grow together or grow apart – the emphasis here upon *growth*. And we can relate this to our experiences in organizational life too. Stagnation - going nowhere; the same ol' same ol' - causes so much unhappiness, so much dissatisfaction, so much boredom (even when there's lots to do!!) and lack of fulfillment.

If leadership and management are about dealing with people; if business is about relationships; if everything you do is implemented through people, then working on those relationships becomes a priority.

Interact and Engage

Since organizations consist of networks spawning additional networks, any failure on your part to plug into some of these merely constitutes getting in your own way. The days of command structures and organizational hierarchy being the true controlling and informational highways are coming to an end. To have influence, insight, and knowledge, you will have to interact and engage with the key entities in social networks: the people!

Working for *Them*

Think carefully over what it is you are trying to do. An organization hires capable people to do a job. It then becomes your job to make certain they perform and deliver. But that's just the surface management stuff. Outside of the visible and rigid managerial role – reports, structures, procedures – there is the more fluid boundary-less leadership element: you do all you can to make sure the managers and the organization get out of the way of the people trying to do the job they were hired to do.

When you interact and engage and communicate with people you have appointed to do tasks, you are, in effect, moving into the subtle position of you working for *them*. They work for the organization, you work for them to streamline and smoothen out how things are done – you are the obstacle remover.

This is not some hippy notion or feel-good guru nonsense: when you switch from left-brained structured management into right-brained leadership activities and behavior, you must always see yourself as working for those you seek to lead. This right-brained leadership later enables you to correct or improve upon the rigid managerial reports, structures, and procedures thereby enabling you to lock-in a newer improved left-brained managerial system of operations: you work for them, you deliver results to them and in turn the organization or department or team improves and everyone, including you, succeeds. This, it is hoped, then enables the desired organizational culture and employee style of behavior to flourish; you have set a suitable example, others can follow it, and you now have an improved system of reports and metrics to lock-in the new behavior.

Keep this in mind always: when you flick into leadership mode, you are working for *them*.

Don't Let an Employee Neutralize You

"Listen sonny, I've got kids older than you are. Don't come in here with your head full of college books thinking you can wave your magic wand and make everything okay – this is the real world".

An employee saying something along those lines is out to neutralize you, even if they wouldn't use that particular term themselves. Or maybe they'll say something like, *"Listen, I've worked here for more than twenty years. You don't know this company. Hell, I heard you never even worked in this industry before!"*

Your first step to managing this situation is recognizing it for what it is.

Your second step is to know that domination, or intimidation, or competition, or shame in needing help, or fear of looking weak – or a combination of all these things – is lurking in the background within the employee's psyche whether he or she actually recognizes this or not.

Third, notice what it is any employee behaving in this way is really doing. By neutralizing their manager, they are neutralizing your ability to help or hurt them. So they empower themselves and feel better by disempowering *you*. Or so they think. In truth, they are preventing you from helping them.

Fourth, don't make the mistake of launching a counterattack aimed at one-upmanship. You should not feel under threat. Whenever anyone tries this out on me, I sit back and can't help but smile because I can see precisely what is going on. As a result, I become even more cool, calm, and collected. This in itself causes me to exude confidence and a sense of control thereby immediately signaling to the person trying to neutralize me that it's not working.

"So what makes you conclude, before I even say a word, that I could never help you in a million years?" or *"Why do you think me coming from another industry equals 'he can't help me?'"* Calm reactive questioning like this gets straight to the point. Remember, by asking questions, you give yourself the opportunity to go into listening mode. See if you can tease out their logic. Very often, it's not very logical at all. Very often an employee will not be fully aware of the effect his behavior has on the people around him. *"Is that your opening sentence to every manager who wants to have a chat with you?"* is the type of thing you may consider bouncing back to them.

An employee who is trying to neutralize you simply wants to shut you up. They don't want dialogue unless it's entirely on *their* terms. But if you ask question after question, and keep digging until you find out what this guy's problem really is, you'll be helping yourself, the employee, the business, the people who have to work beside him everyday and maybe even his family at home too! And, as I always remind people, sometimes the troublemakers *do* have a point; they may simply be locked mentally into a previous bad experience with a previous manager or a previous poor organizational context – sometimes your job becomes one of unlocking them rather than unwittingly ditching a valuable contributor to the organization.

Collaboration and Mutual Interdependence

> One of the most important ways to establish a strong working alliance with [employees] is to work together collaboratively – as partners...one of the [manager's] primary aims is to articulate clear expectations for working in this collaborative manner and, more importantly, to enact behaviorally these spoken expectations by giving [employees] the *experience* of working together on their problems.[37]

Collaboration and Mutual Interdependence as it will appear throughout this book is not some soppy notion. Keep that in mind. You have a business or division or department or team to run.

You cannot escape what we covered in book 1: *every*body sets an example. It is for you, exercising leadership, to set a suitable example. Doing so breaks down barriers, gets you noticed, gets people talking, builds trust, and – over time – generates buy-in and commitment.

There is collaboration in structured conversation. This is why asking questions is so powerful: it shows you're interested. It allows people to sound-off for a while. Ignore the tone at first, and you'll notice some very valuable information coming at you wrapped in some very powerful emotions. Those powerful emotions exist for a reason – go find out why!

> You must replace judgment with empathy, and lectures with questions. If you do so, you gain influence. The instant you stop trying to impose your agenda on others, you eliminate the fight for control. You sidestep irrelevant battles over whose view of the world is correct...When you listen and they talk, they discover on their own what they must do.[38]

---

[37] Teyber (2006) p. 45. Square brackets added here. "Employee" has been inserted in place of "client" and "manager" inserted in place of "therapist".
[38] Patterson et al (2008) p. 105.

66

Effective Listening

Note the thread running through everything we are covered so far: Trust! Several times I have mentioned people should not fear the possibility of being punished for speaking up. The second thread is this: consistency (a key theme in *If You Cannot Manage Yourself, You Cannot Manage Others*). When you are consistent in person; consistent in enforcement; consistent in your decision making style, trust arrives of its own accord - actions *always* speak louder than words.

Some say 'Active Listening,' others will tell you 'Empathetic Listening' – the key point, however, should be this: find out what the person is saying, what they actually mean, how they really feel about the issue and what this all comes down to in their world. Only by understanding from their perspective can you see how to communicate back to them in a truly effective way.

Don't listen simply to confirm your own views or to gather evidence to dismiss them. Make sure you silence the internal monologue running through your own brain – always start with You! Don't blindly mimic their words back to them as some active listening techniques might cause you to do. A parrot can mimic but has no idea what it is saying – so, don't be a parrot! Instead, rephrase it to them to see if they agree you heard them correctly. Don't just juggle the words around: rephrase the feelings and emotions to get at what is really going on.

Effective listening can be tiring at first. You need to build up what I term your "listening fitness". It also requires patience. Yes, you will certainly have to keep the employee on point and stop them rambling off on tangents, but they will ramble a bit. If dealing with an angry employee, customer, or client, let them talk out their frustration. If you interrupt them, the conversation will go on all day. They'll defend and argue every point. While you talk, they focus on their next point or countering your previous point: they won't be listening. Instead, let them talk everything out and then you can deal with everything in one fell swoop.

The point is to use *upfront* effective listening. Don't wait for a problem to arise. Manage by walking around. Interact with people. Go find out for yourself. Upfront effective listening can help you avoid a lot of problems you might not otherwise have seen coming. It also allows you to hear what your direct reports – the middle men and women; the barriers between you and the front lines – may not be telling you or what they may have watered down when communicating to you. As I have said to countless managers over the years: numbers will tell you what, but rarely *why*! Talking to people reveals the 'why' part; and knowing the 'why' part upfront can avoid so much difficulty later.

Use structured conversation but don't ask habit questions. By this I mean don't ask the same people the same predictable unimaginative questions or you'll become predictable and the employees' answers will become automatic. Worse, employees may start to use your laziness in this regard against you. Don't put your answers in the questions. This dis-empowers you. You know the sort of questions: "How come you were late this morning – was the traffic bad?" Unless you know the traffic was *not* bad and you're out to trap the person, such questions offer them a way out without any thinking.

Maintain eye contact; watch your body language; keep the employee on point; ask questions as a form of clarifying what you are hearing and of helping to lead the employee to solutions and discoveries for themselves. Remember, employees very often know things or have insights into issues you don't even know exist.

Preliminary Questions to Break the Ice and Gain Commitment

When a new issue gets kicked up to you, or if you are new in your role, you need to ask questions and then employ Effective Listening to what an employee says back to you. Consider asking the following questions:[39]

- How have other managers or supervisors responded to you in the past when you have asked for help?
- Do you think your experience will be the same or different with me?
- If you and I begin to work on some of the problems you're having out there, what do you think might go wrong between us?
- What might *I* do to make things worse if you agree to let me help you?

These questions enable you to assess where the employee is coming from, what their fears and reservations might be. They also enable you to demonstrate that you are willing to accept that it could very well be *you* who will foul things up and make things worse; you're admitting you're only human and not infallible. By asking these things, you can tailor your approach, gain an insight into their perspective, and reframe and rework everything to ensure you make your own job so much easier in the long run.

How to Get Value from Interactions

Statements like, "I'm fine", or "Everything's going okay, I guess", tell you nothing of any value. For the lazy manager,

---

[39] These questions are taken from (albeit slightly altered) Teyber (2006) p. 90.

however, such statements are a license to keep walking: so long as there aren't any problems, great!

People will only talk if you stamp out fear. This is why an ability to manage yourself first is key. The last thing you want to do when an employee tells you something is to rush straight to action. You may go off half-cocked. You may not have the full story or all the facts. You may make the employee look like he's ratting someone out. If you do any of these things, if you lose your temper, belittle the employee or dismiss their views, you're killing off their motivation to ever talk with you again. So manage YOU – always start with YOU – first!

You *must* become a champion for clarity. But clarity must move in all directions hence my advice to you that you get employees comfortable with asking *you* questions too. A lack of clarity only makes a problem worse.

You must take seriously whatever matters to the employee – however daft this may seem to you at first. Refusing to deal with such instances does not mean the employee does not carry things through to their illogical conclusion.

Try not to focus too heavily on the past. A brief overview, a list of the previous solutions attempted is about all you need. You don't want your conversations to descend into a blame-game postmortem that does little to move you forward.

There is also a need to ensure you don't spend too much time talking about things the employee can do nothing about – unless of course they can't do anything because *you* are unnecessarily getting in their way. Instead, get them to focus on making things better. Thinking too much about what they have lost or can do nothing about simply encourages a problem-oriented mindset – something you don't want. It also dampens their mood by introducing helplessness and pessimism rather than a solution-oriented mindset and a willingness to brainstorm, experiment, and move forward.

Make bad points a footnote to praise and not the other way around. But don't say something positive and then add a "but" to the middle of the sentence. We've already seen what happens when you do that. Instead, give the praise and then suggest steps to even better improvement. For example, "You handled that client very well and I think you could go one better by maintaining greater eye contact the next time". That's so much better than "You handled that client very well but I don't think you were very good on the eye contact. You'll need to watch that next time".

Many counselors who deal with children will advise that negative feedback be delivered in ten words or less in order to be effective, retain focus, and to add clarity: preparation and up-front thinking are therefore the order of the day.

Don't sit around waiting to correct them. Instead try to catch them doing something right.[40] Praise the parts they get right thereby reinforcing the desired behavior. Have patience. You need to encourage people along, grow their confidence, keep them moving in the right direction. Just be aware of viewing yourself as "nurturing" when *they* may see you as "micro-managing". Let them know you'll check in every once in a while. Once they get things right, walk away and leave them to it: get out of their way!

Finally, always make sure you leave the person, or they leave your office, in a positive, proactive or searching frame of mind. I would recommend that you watch the clock and then spend the last 25% of the time available building up the person you are talking with. Thank them for their input. Let them know their input is valuable and their suggestions welcome. Give them a label to live up to: express confidence in their ability; let them know *you* know they are better than the problem or issue. Get them to agree to achieve something positive in the interval

---

[40] A concept put forward and advocated by Blanchard et al (2004).

before seeing them again: something that will move them forward rather than cause them to dwell on past failures or become frustrated with their current position. If you don't, you're only creating further problems for yourself to manage in the future.

> In traditional counseling, a lot of time is spent both inquiring into and listening to clients complain about their symptoms, the actions of other people, the world they live in, and on and on – the list is endless. The more they are encouraged or allowed to do so, the more important the complaints become...the only persons we can control are ourselves. We can't control anyone else, including our counselors, with these complaints.[41]

Don't Allow the Tail Wag the Dog

When a worker tells you the two or three main obstacles standing in their way of being happy at work or from doing a good job, work together to examine and remedy these. It's as simple as that. Manage the conversation. You're not there to listen to demands or take ultimatums. You're there to figure out what's going on and to then assist in the creation of a solution to the benefit of all.

To maintain a sense of control, it is often best *not* to go back to an employee immediately or even the same or next day. People often become overly emotional on issues; after all, they finally worked up the courage to tell you what they think so it's probably got a lot of underlying angst or aggression lurking just beneath the surface.

Let their blood cool a little. Also, taking your time to revert to them enables you retain your status: returning too soon can often see respect or aura crumble. It may be unfashionable to point out, but familiarity does breed a certain level of contempt. Where possible, delay slightly in going back to a person so that the sense of *them* controlling you does not arise.

---

[41] Glasser (1998) p. 117.

Stay on Topic

Even with all the technology around us, I refuse to work anywhere that doesn't have whiteboards or the like up on the walls. As a person talks to me but then goes off on a tangent, I will write the tangent up on a board off to the side of the room, but then tell them to get back on topic. Seeing it on the board assures them that it will *not* be forgotten.

Doing this saves me a lot of time. It enables me manage the conversation and get to where we need to get to. It shows the other person that I will not be distracted from getting to what I want to get at.

But it also, over time, teaches people who meet with me regularly to manage what *they* say too. After a while, you'll even find one or two people standing up and writing a point on one of the boards on the side of the room without saying anything. This is when you know you are being effective as a manager and the person with you is learning and improving. They have started to manage their own conversation, have learned to stay on point, are not sidelining important but not-so-relevant-right-now points, and are not assuming they can take up all of your time as and when they please.

Turn Confrontation into Support

There is a difference between confronting someone and being in conflict with them. Confrontation should not lead to all out war. Maturity on the part of both parties should ensure this. If I think you don't fully understand something, I'll confront you: "You seem to be doing things the wrong way around. Let me show you..." - I've spotted a problem in your performance and I've confronted you over it. My style ensures you do not feel threatened or humiliated so my confrontation does not become conflict.

Confronting someone can also be a form of support. Support is very important in today's world. Too many of us feel lost. Too many of us have to meet tough metrics and can very often feel alone in our endeavor. As in the example above, instead of standing idly by and watching you continually doing something the wrong way, I have intervened as a form of support thereby avoiding you getting into trouble later.

Some of the key ingredients common to all forms of psychotherapy are genuineness, empathy, and positive regard.[42] In leadership and management, none of this should be a surprise to you given everything we have covered so far. We may not have used these labels, but you *should* recognize them. We have already mentioned the idea of catching people doing something right. We have seen the importance of listening to people, of not reacting and making them sorry they ever spoke in the first place.

As a manager, if you are not genuine you *will* be found out sooner or later. If you lack empathy – an ability to understand how an employee subjectively experiences the things he talks about – you cannot hope to build trust, buy-in, or commitment. And if you lack positive regard for the employee – if you simply don't care – then they *will* pick up on this and your job will instantly become more difficult.

The "Child-Friendly Elevator Pitch"

I always tell people that simplicity and genius walk hand-in-hand. There is no need to become overly complicated in leading and managing people. Just keep things simple.

It is not just for you the manager to ask questions: teach employees to do the same. Instead of walking away not sure of

---

[42] For greater discussion on this point, see: Scaturo (2005).

what is going on, they need to know to ask questions thereby making both *their* lives and *your* job so much easier.

You need to teach people to come to the point. There's nothing more frustrating than someone dancing around the edges. Get them to develop what I term the "Child Friendly Elevator Pitch". This is simply a short, sharp statement of what the problem is in terms even a child would understand. Just like a sales pitch, an employee should be able to step into an elevator with you on any given floor and have communicated to you precisely what the problem is by the time you step out on your destination floor: the Child Friendly Elevator Pitch.

Get the Employee Involved

Collaboration and Mutual Interdependence means precisely that: the employee can't just sit on his ass waiting for you to solve everything for him. The truth is, very often, you yourself will not have the first clue how to resolve the issue – it's a fact of leadership and management, so get used to it!

Ask him whether or not he has tried to remedy his predicament before. Ask him to list all the things he has tried in the past. What does he think works for him and why? What have others done? What does he think you and he can do now? This approach will help both of you, particularly when you yourself are unsure how to proceed.

Asking questions that get the employee involved brings focus on where his locus of control may rest – does he seem internal or external locus of control? Do you get the impression he is too quick to blame and duck responsibility or accountability? Does he seem problem-oriented in mindset or solution-oriented?

You have to make him see that if he does not make suggestions to make his own life easier then blame *will* migrate to *him*. His complaining will not constitute suitable example setting to everyone around him if he refuses an offer to help himself.

Speak *Their* Language

When seeking to build a relationship with employees, it is important that you speak *their* language. But you can't know what that language is until you listen to them for a while and get to know them. If you find that one worker likes baseball, then you'll get through to him so much easier when you start using baseball analogies. As with everything else, however, be genuine and know what it is you're talking about otherwise you'll do more harm than good.

But we can go deeper. By listening, we can answer in the right language. Psychologically, speaking their language gives you a direct line into their brain. If an employee says something like, "That doesn't sound right", you could reply with "I hear what you're saying. I'll talk to R&D and make all the right noises to make sure this stuff clicks together in time". The employee used "sound" so I respond in the same language with "hear", "noises", "clicks". If it was the employee who loves baseball, I could go farther by mixing analogy with language: "I hear what you're saying. Don't want anything coming at us out of left field just before the final innings. I'll get on to R&D and make the right noises to ensure this thing clicks together for us".

See what's happening here? By taking the time to get to know people – frontloading your efforts – simple interactions become so much easier to manage. Even unforeseen problems or resistance can be managed because you have the ability to instantly plug into the language this person operates on thereby making your job easier. You convey the impression of knowing what *they're* talking about. You build trust by replying in *their* language and you are so much more persuasive (leading is mostly persuasion) because of this.

Set Out the Roadmap

When dealing with people, if you can get *them* to suggest hitching posts along the way, they'll buy into what you're trying to do far more easily than if *you* hand down to them what they are to do - again, our mutual interdependence and collaborative approach. Often, you *are* handing a course of action down to them: allowing *them* to suggest the pertinent points takes a little more time but generates a lot more progress in the end. So let *them* suggest your own directions for you.

When meeting with an employee on any given issue, it is for the *manager* to structure the meeting as much as possible and to provide the employee with guidelines and direction for what is going to occur in the meeting –

> "Tom, I want to chat with you about the difficulties you seem to be having making your targets. I'll spend the first two minutes outlining the figures for the past three-months. Then I want *you* to tell *me* where you think the problems lie. After that, we'll spend the majority of our time together agreeing on steps we think both you and I should take to help you get back on track. You're better than your results indicate and I want the two of us to fix this before it becomes a *real* problem. Does that sound okay to you?"

While not the perfect set of sentences, the desired impact should be clear. I'm confronting Tom but in a *non*-threatening way. I have assured him that he is *not* in trouble. I have given him something to live up to by telling him that he knows he is better than his results are showing. I've told him precisely what is coming in this get-together. He knows he must listen to me first. He then sees that I will listen to him in return, from which my sense of genuineness, empathy for his predicament and positive regard for him as a person will come across. He sees that this is a two-way process and not simply me laying down the law or handing him the solution on a plate. He has direct input and gets instantaneous feedback on what he is saying. Most importantly, he sees that there are next steps and return meetings in the near future.

Far too many managers set out to help but then become too busy. The end result – they have one or maybe two worthwhile conversations and then that's about it. If you're too busy to chat with your employees you shouldn't be trying to lead or manage!

Get Out of Their Way

It is truly amazing how often we expect people to do something while at the same time standing in their way of doing it.

We impose so many rules, procedures, metrics, that we build walls across the roads we want our employees to travel down. Take large retail stores as an example. Employees are expected to push membership cards on customers and yet many retailers don't have screens facing the customers or, if they do, data that helps the customer want to *buy* rather than the employee have to *sell*: Retailers set targets but then get in the way of their employees reaching those targets. Then the managers spend lots of time managing the symptoms i.e. missed targets, rather than the causes – systems that get in the way or just don't help.

Poor or vague instructions constitute getting in their way. As a manager, you need to be specific. Don't say something vague like "do better next time," or, "Hey, everybody, look at

the wonderful comments a customer emailed us about John in the
Customer Service Department." Neither of these comments gives the 'how' for improving outcomes – they give the warning or the recognition, but not the 'how' part.

In order to steer behavior, you need to be specific: set a target; work together to formulate steps they should consider taking; show how they differ in approach from that of the successful deviant in the department; give them a timeframe for getting there; give them resources; give them feedback along the way – particularly praise and encouragement.

Hire smart people and then get out of their way. Stifle their creativity - get in their way too often - and employees may leave to work for a competitor or, worse still, to set up a competing business. Remember what I said earlier: a little selfishness can be very healthy; by getting out of *their* way, you get out of *your* way!

Check In Regularly

Don't just ramble on, conclude, and then wrap things up. Leave time at the end to build the employee up. Praise them for their good points and qualities. Thank them for their time, but always "check in".

Checking in is a way of ensuring the employee is still with you and also a way of determining whether or not their attitude has softened toward you. In this regard, it also enables *them* to see how their perspective is changing.

Toward the end of a one-to-one discussion, ask questions like:

- Did you find this meeting productive?
- Are you starting to view things differently?

- Are you happy now with how I'm going about this?
- You seemed very resistant when I first brought this topic up – how do you feel now?

Check in regularly. Maintain a feel for how you are progressing. Show the employee that you are not a monster operating to your own selfish agenda: *manage* your meetings.

Smile

Remember what we're talking about here in this chapter: *building* the relationship. You'll hardly melt the ice with a cold stare or by looking away from people as you come into contact with them. Doing so pulls down relationships or prevents them from ever becoming of benefit. In today's problem-burdened world of busy and irritable people, the smile has become seriously underrated.

A smile can be an ice breaker. Remember, first impressions last for quite a while. But it *must* be genuine. We all know when someone is faking it. I'm not talking about a huge pose-like smile that makes your face sore: a simple easy smile will do.

When I came to America I had to work at the ground level in retail. It was amazing just how far a simple smile got me everyday. I became quite popular. Just a "Hi" with a tiny smile suggesting I didn't hate being there and wasn't disappointed to see them!

Of course, every once in a while you'll meet an ass who reacts by frowning and looking away. Such people are in the minority. Don't let them ruin your day. Managing such people becomes interesting. Don't react. Let it slide at first and then see if, over a few days, your greeting to them elicits a different reaction. If not, it's probably time you had a chat with that person.

Express Appreciation and Thanks

Again, as with smiling, be genuine. There's no need to strike up the band and have streamers falling from the sky; a simple thanks will get you a long way.

In retail, whenever a manager came to the cash register, for example, to do something for me requiring their security code, I always thanked them even though it was part of their job. I know for certain that simply doing that got me so much farther in terms of the likeability factor with them than anything else.

But sometimes we feel awkward thanking a person. It feels like expressing weakness so instead we hope they'll get that we're grateful. It's always better to say it just to be sure. Plus, it's no more than right to thank someone for doing you a good turn.

Praise

Some managers can feel very awkward giving praise. It makes them feel embarrassed and they're afraid of how the employee might react. They may even feel they're kiss-assing or crawling to the employee. As I have stated time and time again – if you cannot manage yourself you cannot manage others.

As with most other things in leadership and management, praise must be genuine and come from opinions sincerely held. If not, you *will* be found out.

In truth, if you praised a little more you wouldn't have to give out as many pay raises as you do: praise can enable you to switch from extrinsic to intrinsic motivation in employees. Or, in simple English – praise has a lower cost.

Some Final Thoughts

A failure on your part as manager to assess what is really going on and to spend time building collaborative and mutually interdependent relationships will simply see you spending your time managing all the consequences of not doing these things – it's as simple as that. Your Choice not to do things properly will create extra Demands of you and you'll be operating under unnecessary Constraints as a result.

Build your top team. Assess them. Determine whether or not they have the right attitudes, mindsets, abilities, and interpersonal skills to get you to where you want to go. Be ruthlessly honest: get this team wrong and you're dead. They must be loyal to *the team* first and not the people in their silos. Rotate faces in and out of this top team throughout your tenure; the people who got you here may not be as capable as some of the new people you hired recently at getting you to the next stage – that old mantra: what got you here won't get you there.

You need clear and effective communication, a willingness to listen to people from outside the top team, and a willingness to engage in healthy and productive confrontation when necessary.

Get everyone in the business talking to you. Get them listening. Ask for suggestions and solutions. Show you are willing to listen. Make it crystal clear that nobody will be punished for having the courage to participate and contribute. When *you* talk, speak *their* language.

Don't allow yourself to be distracted by tangents and side issues. Pick a topic, retain focus, resolve to reach a definitive conclusion with clear action steps to be taken by individuals within set time periods.

None of your interacting with employees is about you surrendering power, authority, or credibility. Don't let people neutralize you. Manage your interactions with them. Stay on point. Don't accept ultimatums. Don't be bullied or harassed into anything. Steer clear of focusing on negatives only. Make it abundantly clear through your tone and attitude that you expect solution-oriented mindsets focused on long-term solutions.

Always select people with personal credibility who will support you and who the workers trust. Select people who conform to your values – interview them to your list of organizational cultural values. There's no point hiring someone and then spending years trying to change them. Hire in the change you want to take place.

But bear in mind that you don't need all the great values. A small number of focused and concentrated ones are enough. A shopping list of what all the gurus tell you works is not the way to go. A small number of values that go right to the heart of the organizational culture you want to create and the behavior you want employees to exhibit is all that is required: *Good Enough*! Remember, simplicity and genius walk hand-in-hand.

Chapter 4

Invisible Impactors

The Little Things that Make a BIG Difference

Too much of our time is spent managing the things we can see; the things that are capable of representation on the Income and Balance Sheets - on the obvious things. Remember, numbers will tell you what, but rarely why.

Our business students are taught to read books and analyze case studies while not being taught how to read people or lead or manage them effectively; simply put: business school does *not* teach you how to lead or manage people. Our attitude seems to be: look after the numbers and everything else will look after itself. As we are starting to see, however, there are really three options: (1) Attend to the numbers; (2) Attend to the people; (3) Do it *all*, but in the right way.

Some Not-So-Obvious Truths

People are *always* motivated. Most of the time, however, they are just not motivated to do what the organization needs them to do. This is your challenge; their remaining this way will, in time, become your potential failure.

People are *always* creative. But they generally work for organizations where the managers and prevailing organizational cultures are so restrictive that they practice their creativity outside of the work setting. What a waste!

People are always watching and listening and thinking and feeling. This is why the Five Constituencies (see below) and my definition of an organization as a 'social' network is of crucial importance; remember: everything done, not done, said, not said, causes people to watch and listen. This leads to my next point.

People are always talking; they're always communicating – is it good or bad? Constructive or destructive? Through the Five Constituencies and out to customers and stakeholders – is what they are communicating helpful or hindering to the organization?

Money is not a very good motivator. Oh sure, it's a great attractor but, over time, its power to retain will diminish. This is because money is simply *one* slice of the overall motivational pie. Other slices have labels like, "sense of achievement", "sense of purpose", "ability to grow", "feel like I belong", "feel like I'm developing" – and other such things. But it is your individual perspective on money and your life situation that determines just how big a slice of the pie money becomes. For example; if you got married tomorrow, took out a new mortgage, and started having a family, you can bet the money slice of the pie would suddenly expand in size. Conversely; imagine your manager is an idiot who never appreciates all the brilliant things you did this year and all the times you saved his worthless ass - over time, all the money in the world couldn't stop you leaving.

Key Ingredients

Remember, there are Five Constituencies you need to keep in mind when observing behavior and when seeking to manage people in an effective way.

Take a look at the diagram below that appeared in Book One of this series.[43]

The Five Constituencies are:

1. The person you are observing;
2. The people around them;
3. The company/business/organization as a whole;
4. External Stakeholders;
5. You.

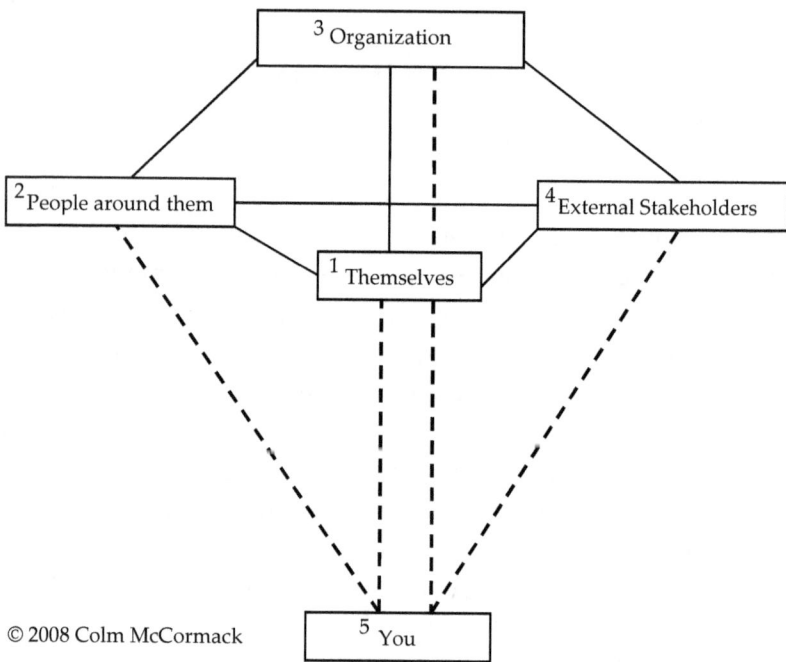

© 2008 Colm McCormack

As you will see, the person under observation is placed at the heart of the diagram with firm lines of connection to and from the people around them, the organization, and external

---

[43] For a full discussion on the Five Constituency Model for Observing Behavioral Impact, see book 1 in this series: *If You Cannot Manage Yourself, You Cannot Manage Others* - McCormack (2008) chapter 1 and/or visit: www.JustManageIt.com

stakeholders. You, however, are slightly removed due to you exercising observation and therefore are not actively taking part or allowing yourself to be influenced by proceedings. The lines connecting you with the other four main constituencies are depicted as dashed to represent your awareness through observation of what is going on. In other words, you are aware and you choose what you will allow affect you and the extent of such affects.

Holding these Five Constituencies within your contemplation allows you to see the big picture. You can see what is really going on and how many people may be impacted by any actions you take or don't take, the things you say or don't say. This enables you to manage intelligently. You can deal with one person while at the same time ensuring that your interventions prevent undesirable consequences spreading out to any of the other Constituencies: when dealing with one person you ignore the network at your peril!

Now, we need to look at the factors that impact upon the behavior of those Five Constituencies.

Remember, your aim is to *understand* behavior. If you simply rush out and start managing it there is no guarantee you will get things right or that you will prevent problems from reoccurring:[44]

---

[44] Taken from Book 1: McCormack (2008), chapter 6.

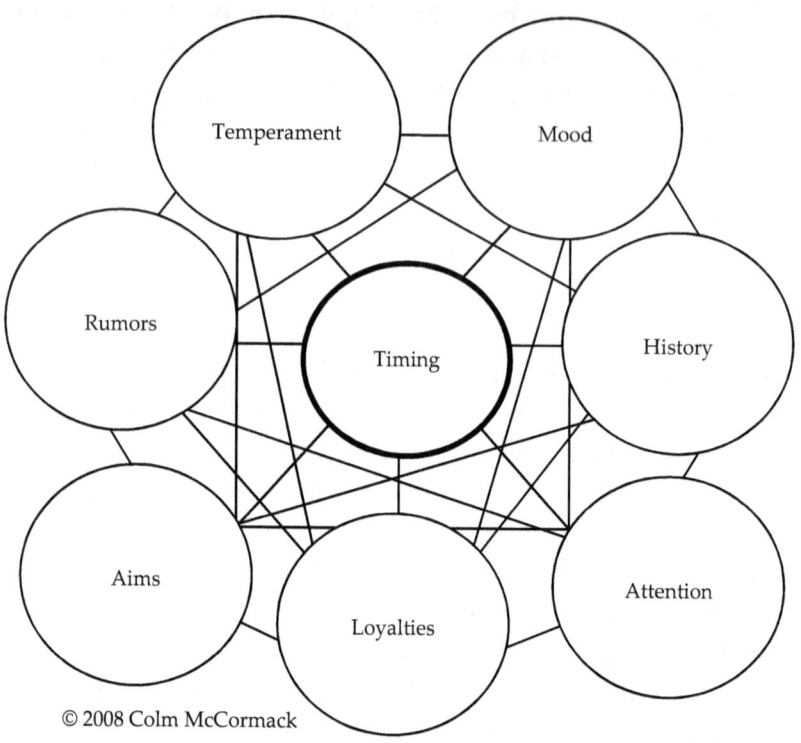

© 2008 Colm McCormack

Note how all the factors are interrelated – there are lines joining each with every one of the others.

The following table now gives a brief insight into each of the factors:

Mood	A person's mood is a huge determinant in how they react to a given thing at any given moment.
History	What is this person's history with the business? How have they reacted before? Is there a pattern? Are they predictable? Have they shown signs of flexibility or willingness to change?
Attention	Do they care about the topic you are focusing on? You'll need to alter your approach depending on whether they're paying attention or not. You may even have to deliberately do a thing in such a way that it does or does not come to their attention.

Loyalties	Where might their loyalties lie? Can you confirm this? Might anything change their perspective or expected reaction?
Aims	Does this person have any major projects, goals, targets that they want to achieve? Do they want their own store or own division? Do they want to get rid of a colleague, change the IT system – anything?
Rumors	People react to rumors. They may only raise their guard, but it's a reaction nonetheless. If there are rumors going around that could help or hinder you, plug into them and use them to your advantage or alter your approach to sidestep their effect.
Temperament	Is this an angry or shy person? Do they jump to conclusions, fly off the handle, or are they slow, thoughtful, methodical?
Timing	Timing is the key to all the others. Approach someone when they're in the wrong mood to receive what you're saying, and you'll fail. If you know their aims, you can play to these and perhaps even help them achieve some of them along the way. If you know their temperament, you can manipulate them to lose their temper, to jump straight to action, to stall – whatever: depends on their individual temperament. You can use rumor, loyalty and history to your advantage too. Remember, it's not always what you need to do that counts: it's also the order in which you do them and when: *Timing*.

Everything here is interrelated. Your history with an organization will determine the things you want to achieve, the people and things you are loyal to, how you react to rumors. The same for any one of the factors: each has a ripple-effect across all the others. It is for *you* to determine the strength of impact upon each factor and manage this to suit what you are trying to do. This is why engaging with people by walking around, holding continual ongoing conversations, and building collaborative and mutually interdependent relationships are key steps toward truly effective leadership and management. Without these steps you won't have a clue of the rumors, loyalties, aims, temperament, of each person in the business. An absence of frontloading your efforts will see you implementing the wrong things in the wrong way and then having to deal with the consequences of such outcomes: poor upfront Choices creating unnecessary Demands of yourself thereby forcing you to operate under self-enforced Constraints; all totally unnecessary – laziness *never* pays: it *always* costs!

Negativity

In many ways, this is one of the most invisible forces impacting people every day. So much of the quality of our lives and how much we achieve is dictated by the people around us: we saw this in book 1.

Observe your employees closely on an ongoing basis: don't spy, simply pay attention. Who do they get their news and insights from? What is the tone of the person or people conveying these insights and opinions? Is there a small clique of regular nay-sayers polluting everything around them because no-one dares stand against them?

> Dismissing people as cranks and crackpots, while ignoring their potential to cause serious damage, is not effective management.[45]

Negativity spreads and it spreads fast. It doesn't recognize the delineation between different departments or divisions or ranks within an organization. Once it gets a hold, it can be extremely difficult to shake off. Remember what we saw earlier: not all negative people come across as negative.

Here's a question for you: what do you think is the ratio of positive to negative statements the average person hears both at home and at work in any given day? Which do you think occurs the most – negative or positive statements? If you don't know, go find out. Research on the topic reveals some very depressing results indeed.

---

[45] From Book 1: McCormack (2008).

Organizational Culture

This is not intended to be a full discussion on organizational culture – please visit my website (www.JustManageIt.com) for a more in-depth discussion. There are, however, some key points that cannot go unmentioned.

First; think of any organizational culture as having three possibilities: (1) what they say it is; (2) what it actually is; (3) what it needs to be. With these three factors in mind, it is just amazing how delusional some key players in an organization sound when talking about the organizational culture they 'say' exists on the ground.

Second; organizational culture is shared learned behavior – it has history and experience. Never forget this. It is more than a label or a definition: it is history; stories; experiences; learning; steps and missteps and good and bad stories all rolled into one overall outcome that dictates the types of behaviors people will and will not engage in.

Third; the organizational culture of any building you walk into is often quite easy to label – but it is the 'why' that is the hard part. Why is that particular culture in place and why did it stick and why does it continue to prevail and why doesn't it change? Again, not knowing that culture is a shared learned behavior over a long period of time will bar you from discovering the 'why'.

Fourth; organizational culture initiatives and talks and projects are often mere passing fads in the minds of managers until something more pressing presents itself – usually some set of numbers not being met! Since culture is a long-term shared learned behavior, you know that changing it must also take a long and sustained effort too.

Fifth; changing organizational culture requires focused, ongoing and unrelenting discipline. As you know by now, the only way to change behavior is: (1) set the example/model the behavior; (2) incentivize the desired behavior; (3) install the correct metrics to guide...

I would recommend you create a culture in which people are expected to ask questions - a culture where they feel free to ask and safe to ask. It should be a culture of collaboration. This does not mean time wasted chatting about nonsense, moaning all day long or bitching or backstabbing.

You'll get a very clear insight into the type of organizational culture in place in your organization or division simply by doing everything we have discussed so far: observe, analyze, talk to people and listen to what they're saying.

Draw up a list of the qualities you would expect a person suited to that type of culture to have. Then, when ever you hire new people, base your recruitment criteria along those qualities.

Get rid of the people who will not play to where you want to move the company. Seek out and lock-in those who have been desiring and advocating the changes you want to bring about; they will be your supporters and enablers.

Your organizational culture must allow mistakes. It must allow for what I term "intelligent experimentation" and "intelligent failure". Your organizational culture *must* allow for learning from mistakes, learning from failures, learning from successes, and spreading that knowledge throughout the business for everyone to learn. Such a culture should promote solution-oriented mindsets in all employees, not problem-oriented ones. Remember, Collaboration and Mutual Interdependence is your goal: clear and effective communication will be your enabler.

Bureaucracy

Bureaucracy is *not* a monster. Modern business gurus and the media have us all afraid of this one: bureaucracy is bad, it slows things down, it's why everything around here sucks – so goes the logic.

But this logic is incorrect. Bureaucracy *does* work provided it (1) is managed correctly; (2) is enabling in nature; (3) is of suitable size subject to our principle of Constantly Reassess.

Look at what we have said before. You need to systemize things otherwise chaos and total disorganization will reign. But when you measure things, map processes, put people into certain jobs, introduce goals, targets, metrics, reporting systems, and use these to strive for increased sales, increased market share, lower costs, maximization of shareholder value – you're creating *bureaucracy*. It is inescapable. Rules are bureaucracy. Reporting is bureaucracy. All of these things are set up, run, and managed through bureaucracy.

> Bypassing critical controls is a problem endemic to many small companies...Internet start-ups during the boom years provide the quintessential example in their goal to stamp out bureaucratic encroachments. But how did "bureaucracy busting" work in practice? Unlimited open lines of communication across hierarchical levels created inefficiencies and even a sense of entitlement for lower-level personnel; long hours at work, with few rules, risked burnout and almost certainly generated wasted time; a "no-rules" entrepreneurial atmosphere diffused accountability and responsibility.[46]

Your job is to determine whether there is too much or not enough bureaucracy. Is it helping or hindering? How might you streamline things such that the employees' jobs become easier and faster but you don't hand the keys of the asylum over to the lunatics? You *must* measure. You *must* manage. These things require the *right kind* of bureaucracy.

Bureaucracy is therefore Context Sensitive: circumstances dictate how much you need, how tight and how loose.[47] So,

---

[46] Finkelstein (2004) p. 201-202.
[47] For a more in-depth discussion on Context Intelligence, Context Ignorance, the need to create Context Intelligent Managers, and the importance of Context in general for managers, see book 1 in this series: McCormack (2008) chapter 7.

implement a more enabling and less restrictive way of doing things. No bureaucracy whatsoever will lead to chaos and disorganization. Too much will act as a barrier. *Manage* the bureaucracy: don't let *it* manage *you!*

Trust

Remember what it is you do: you lead and manage in the hope of getting things done through people. If there is no trust, you get less done and therefore cannot do the job you are supposed to be doing. Instead, you end up managing all the obstacles you place in your own path.

The majority of obstacles that stand in any manager's path emanate from the manager himself. Sure, your new employees may be an untrusting bunch because of the behavior of their previous manager, but it is now for you to avoid using that as an excuse.

Show that you are willing to listen, and then listen. Don't do anything that may be perceived as punishing those who make suggestions, or ask questions, or object to ideas. You must allow for constructive and healthy dissent, disagreement, confrontation, and conflict.

> Adaptability requires alternatives. Alternatives require dissenters. So as a management innovator you have to ask yourself, do the management processes in my company encourage dissent, and if not, what can I do to change that?[48]

Don't allow job title to win an argument or debate. The best idea wins *irrespective* of who it was that suggested it or the position they hold in the business.

Don't allow job title to act as a bar to progress. I've seen far too many people halted in their tracks because what they were

---

[48] Hamel (2007) p. 168.

trying to do was "outside" their job description, their department, or job title. I myself, as a lowly worker, was once called aside and told that some of the progress I was making was worrying since it involved areas that were more "the role of the leadership team." Right there and then, I could not escape thinking that such a concern was an appalling example of leadership! But the message was clear: halt your progress; you're off the Reserve; it's something we the leaders were not doing – we're going to stop *you* from making such progress and then revert to *not* doing it ourselves!

Root out any lack of trust and investigate why it exists. Always start with YOU. You may not have caused the lack of trust, but might you be perpetuating it as "one of them" through the systems and processes currently in place? What has caused the lack of trust? Who on your senior team might have caused the problem before and, through your failure to replace them, is perceived to be acting the same way under your new tenure? How do you avoid repeating that cause again? How do you put things right? How long will it take? How many people do you need to help you get the word out on this particular issue?

A lack of trust in your organization can constitute a competitive disadvantage against competitors. If there *is* a lack of trust in your organization, start managing it fast.

Managing Change

As with Organizational Culture, for a more in-depth discussion on Managing Change, please visit my website for assistance/direction.

> ...convincing others to see the world differently isn't easy. In fact, others are very likely to resist your attempts to reshape their views. They may tenaciously hold onto outdated, irrational, or even crazy opinions.[49]

---

[49] Patterson et al (2008) p. 45.

Always remember that you arriving in your new job, taking up your new promotion, or deciding to become a better manager right where you are, equates to change: for you and the people around you.

Change can be slow or it can be sudden. It depends on the context in which you are standing. When changing peoples' behavior and how things are generally done in the business, you may have to spend a long time breaking patterns and habits – some of the change will happen quickly, other parts will take longer. But one thing is certain: make changes when things are going well and you'll implement well thought out changes; sit around allowing the business to become fat and slow, and external events may force half thought-out change upon you.

You don't always need to set down on paper your new "Change Program". You can't simply release a company statement telling people to change their behavior: You must model the behavior; you must get others setting suitable examples too. You must spend a long period of time doing things in the new way otherwise people – creatures of habit – *will* revert to the old behaviors. Then, incentivize the new behaviors and install metrics to track and reward. Conversely, we could say that incentivizing the desired behavior also punishes the old undesired behaviors.

Training is change. Developing people is change. We often resist obvious change very strongly but ignore the more subtle forms like training and development.

If you have sought out like-minded people or brought new supporters onboard, your job of changing the organizational culture becomes so much easier. Having supporters enables you to isolate and/or surround those who object: divided they fall. Placing supporters in charge of teams, projects, divisions, and placing some of their like-minded colleagues along side them boosts their chances for success.

Keep the lines of communication open and keep communicating constantly. When people are anxious, suspicious, or scared, they imagine the worst and then start seeking out evidence to confirm their fears. Don't let a communication vacuum develop.

Be fast on certain points. If you believe the senior management team is the problem, then seek out replacements and move quickly. A long drawn out blood letting will simply cause too much distraction and spread fear throughout the organization. If that happens, then good people as well as bad will start jumping ship.

Be selective when rolling out certain changes. Often it is best to roll out one part of a change program to a part of the business where it will have the greatest impact. The accounts department of most businesses, for example, is the one place where all the others intersect. Starting your change process there could very well see improvements throughout the entire organization by way of efficiency and productivity knock-on effects. If you're lucky, you may even get employees from the other functions watching and then wanting some of that change for themselves before you even set about tackling their expected resistance.

Watch for what I term the "One-Fault Barrier". You will often come across a system that has several flaws in it but as soon as you suggest an alternative someone will reject it for some reason. And that's my point: they'll hold tight to a system full of problems because your alternative has *one* problem. Remember, resistance doesn't have to make a lot of sense!

Finally, have a Get Out Clause. If you accept the need to Constantly Reassess, then this means you must accept the possibility that you – always start with YOU – may have put everyone on the wrong track or the new change has shown up problems you didn't foresee. The best ideas in the world often have to be discarded simply because the outside world or laws or consumer expectations change.

Create Conventional Wisdom

If you as a person were to start hearing the same idea from lots of different people, particularly people whose opinions you respect, you'd be more open to listening to this idea. And this is precisely what I am getting at here.

I once had a boss who quite simply did not have the courage to move. He dithered a lot and just couldn't make a decision: he was never sure. So I started chatting to people who worked with him. Over a period of a month or so, I'd casually drop things into conversations. I found lots of ways of saying the same thing. Then one day, he told me that the way to handle this particular problem is to…

And there it was. The weight of numbers – conventional wisdom – had come home to roost. He was now confident of how to proceed because it was the "correct" way to proceed. And why was it correct? Because the world seemed to accept that this is what a smart manager would do. Of course, the "world" was the small number of people around this guy, but I got what I needed to get done. All it took was a little patience.

You'll often find this with unimaginative managers who are at heart nothing but cowards looking to avoid blame. You often see this with your parents, partner, or someone else close to you too. You suggest a solution to their problem but they don't act upon it. Then a few weeks later they say, "I know what I'm going to do about this". And then they start telling you the solution *you* suggested as if it was hot news or a stroke of genius they had themselves.

Accept that some people need to hear the idea, the pros and cons, from someone else or from more than one person. Put your ego away, let them think they're brilliant, have a little patience while the "conventional wisdom" goes around the block, and then move on to the next issue.

The Power of Outsiders

> ...the people with the boldest and most useful ideas about how to reinvent your company's core management process are probably *not* the folks who are managing those processes right now.[50]

Every company I walk into or come into contact with seems to have alarmingly obvious points upon which they can improve. And I often find myself stunned that nobody in that business can spot these things and do something about them.

One reason for this is because of the old adage – drop a frog into boiling water and he'll jump out; drop him in cold water and heat it up slowly and he'll sit there and boil to death. As the outsider, I'm the one being dropped into the hot water: I can immediately see what is wrong. But the people working there for years have been heating up slowly and will boil to death; tiny mistakes that go unnoticed have a cumulative effect over time.

The question of whether you should promote someone from in-house or from the outside is Context Sensitive. If everything is going great and people are constantly improving, then locking down those improvements and retaining that desired organizational culture becomes key. Very often the best way to do this is to promote people who will champion this culture. If on the other hand, the culture is not what it should be and promoting from within will obviously lock-in all the behaviors you would rather not keep, then bringing in some outsiders is best.

---

[50] Hamel (2007) p. 119.

Outsiders bring fresh perspective. They don't see the world through your eyes, and that's good. They bring new skills, new insights, new ideas. They put others on their toes. They don't arrive with long standing loyalties and are not members of any particular in-house political clique. They ask obvious questions about why things are done the way they are. Outsiders signal to those in-house that change is coming, that things won't stay the same, that their own behavior, skills, or attitude was not what was desired.

Always bear in mind, however, that star performers in one company may arrive to work for you and not retain their shine. There is often a lot more to their performance than the person themselves: a good team, the right resources, different incentive plans. Investigate a little deeper when hiring good people. What do they need to be good? What resources will they require? Will their approach rub their new colleagues up the wrong way?

The Propensity Factor[51]

Scenario one: you're wrapped in the American flag and you are walking toward a fully armed Muslim extremist in Afghanistan. Scenario two: you are dressed exactly the same only this time you're on an American army base walking toward a fully armed American soldier coming the other way.

Both men coming toward you are powerful, well-trained, and well equipped. Both have been to war. Both know how to kill and have indeed killed when necessary. But which one do you think will shoot at you? This is the "Propensity Factor".

In strategy class, business students are told to look at the power or strength of suppliers and buyers, competitors' abilities, and so on. They see a powerful supplier and immediately come

---

[51] Propensity is a topic raised by Porter (1980) chapter 6, yet hardly a point given much emphasis by him or by many professors of strategy.

to conclusions *without* ever asking about that supplier's *propensity* to use his power. On-the-ground experience would tell them immediately whether or not the supplier has the propensity to open fire on sight or salute as he passes by.

Many suppliers are extremely powerful but don't use their power. Many competitors could turn around and squash you but they never do. Many have little or no power but attack you like their lives depended on it. Assessing someone's strengths, powers, or abilities, is not enough; only by knowing these people (or by having a contact who knows them) can you ever assess their *propensity* to use those strengths, powers, or abilities.

And it's the same with leading and managing people. Knowing that someone is creative is not any guarantee that they will use those creative powers at work. Knowing that someone is well connected does not mean you can never interfere with that person – they may not use their connections out of pride, ethics, or decency. Knowledge isn't power until or unless it is used. Money can't buy a person everything if it is never spent. Wonder-drugs don't cure if they're not taken properly. Assessing the Propensity Factor is crucial in any given context.

The "Sleeping Sentry" Syndrome

Laziness *never* pays: it *always* costs – sooner or later. Be on the lookout for managers or supervisors asleep at their post.

We saw this in 2008 in the financial crisis of that year. Much of the oversight was ignored. Put another way: all the oversight and regulation was useless in the hands of people with a low *propensity* to enforce it – the Propensity Factor is what really killed us there.

Watch for this in your organization. Are managers allowing the simple basics to slide? Have they stopped interacting with people? Are workers arriving late, unclean, or becoming undisciplined?

Are shortcuts being taken through the system, particularly in relation to money, legal issues, and customer or client issues? Why have a manager who doesn't manage or only half-manages? It's like getting into a car with a driver who won't steer – it's dangerous!

The Importance of Appearance

Ever have someone say, "Oh wow!" when they see what you're wearing? Clothing is a secret language. It's a two-way street: it has an impact on others *and* on *you*. It can make you feel good or important or powerful as you wear it. This in turn alters your mood and how you behave.

Appearance should be habit; it's about maintaining a minimum standard that does not cause you damage.

Today, some companies and industries insist on dressing casual. Fine – but maintain the simple basics:

- They must shower *every* morning;
- Their clothing must be fresh, clean, and presentable;
- They must brush their teeth;
- There must be no body odor.

Being casual must *never* equate to being less than presentable. If your employees' appearance has a negative impact upon customer or client confidence, you've got problems.

You could be losing business and not even know why, so enforce the simple basics and check up on them regularly. It takes courage to call a person aside and tell them their stink or appearance is turning fellow employees' stomachs and frightening customers away. But this guy *is* costing you money, so deal with him.

Some Final Thoughts

Never forget that very often it is the things you *cannot* see that can hurt you the most: Invisible Impactors!

You should know what the Five Constituencies are and always hold them in your contemplation: you ignore the social network implications of any of your actions/inactions at your peril.

Remain aware of the factors that influence the behavior of the people around you – temperament, mood, history, attention, loyalties, aims, rumors, timing. Knowing these things enables you to manage each person in a specific and tailored way thereby increasing your chances of success.

Remember, you don't always have to announce a huge official change program to bring about substantial and lasting change: your sustained behavior alone can get you off to a very good starting via the modeling of new norms and positive example setting.

If the prevailing conventional wisdom is wrong or non-existent on any given matter, create or change it to reduce resistance.

Constantly monitor the levels of negativity in the organization across all topics. Negativity is a creeping and destructive force if left unmanaged.

Any assessment of strength and power without due consideration of propensity to use such things is an incomplete exercise. Never reach a definitive conclusion until you have gauged the "Propensity Factor".

Chapter 5
Communication

Manage the Communication: Don't Let *it* Manage *You*!

Communication is where it all usually falls apart. Friends going into partnership end up as partners; marriages disintegrate on communication issues; managers and employees hate each other without ever really knowing why or where it all started. People get the wrong messages, mixed signals, their wires crossed, read into what isn't there, jump to conclusions, misread intentions, go nuts when what they expected doesn't materialize from the other person - and more; communication and effective and ineffective behavior go hand in-hand.

Business schools generally relegate communication to the shadows. Effective listening is a skill sorely missing from the curriculum. It involves asking questions, listening to the answers, being certain you unearth what it is they understand – whether correctly or otherwise – about the situation or issue. It's about reflecting back to the person what you think they are feeling and what you've heard from the words they have used, because words can mislead – especially when floating on a strong undercurrent of emotion. It is a proactive investigative style of listening that benefits both the listener and the speaker by getting to the heart of things to ensure demands and constraints are lowered for both parties; no point brilliantly managing the wrong things!

You cannot ever hope to lead or manage in anything approaching a truly effective manner if you cannot understand and manage *your own* communications repertoire – again, always start with You! - and those of the people around you. Spoken words, facial expressions, body language, tone, change in facial color, silence, posture – they all communicate. Mastering communication will see you empower yourself and elevate the organization to a higher level of effectiveness.

Remember; an organization is simply a social network of humans linking to and spawning further social networks. This should emphasize for you the importance of communication; everything you do will go through people.

All Forms of Communication

Since eighty percent or more of your time as a manager is used up communicating or dealing with communications, it makes sense to be aware of all the differing forms of communication.

Silence communicates. Shouting communicates. Listening communicates. Posture and body language communicate. Very often, leaning back in your chair while raising your eyebrows and saying nothing will cause the other person to continue talking to justify what they've just said, or – sometimes – to give away more than they should.

Your clothing communicates. Your surroundings communicate. Facial expressions; doing something; not doing it; firing someone; bringing in an outsider – they all communicate. Use all of these things to your advantage. It's not just about knowing the full range in the human communications repertoire; it's also about *understanding* and *managing* it.

Use the Proper Channels

I have no time for people who live by email. Don't get me wrong here: the majority of my written correspondence goes through the email channel.

But it's people who lead and manage this way that really gets me. The problem with today's workplace is not a *lack* of communication: there's too much of it - and email can be a real culprit on this front. We copy things to everyone, fire around messages all week long. Over time, employees and colleagues become numb to email and start ignoring most of it. But then when something really important goes around, immunity to being carpet-bombed by email sees people ignore the important stuff too.

My own rule is this: if it's important, say it face-to-face. For me, that is the most effective channel for important communications. If that's not feasible, use the telephone or online face-to-face substitute forms of communication. The important point to get here is that an important message is different to all the others so must go a different route in a different way in order to stand out.

As someone looking to lead or manage, you need to know whether each communication should go by way of memo, email, telephone call, video conferencing, privately, by billboard, face-to-face, by letter – what ever. And you need to make sure the people working with you are also choosing the right channels for *their* communications. Part of the answer lies in knowing the people with whom you are communicating. Some only turn on their email once or twice per day. Others live on their cell phones. Some don't have cell phones – imagine that! Some hide behind personal assistants. Others open up in social settings or when sitting with you in their living room at home or while riding along in their car.

Insist on Quality

Too much communication is only part of the problem; *quality* is the other.

Far too many managers spend all day everyday talking and lecturing their employees into submission. Then they'll tell you they're great communicators and constantly keep people up to speed. In reality, however, their "talks" are more diatribe than anything else, totally lacking in inspiration or motivational quality.

Again, this is why it is important that you observe. Many supervisors or team leaders may seek to impress you. Listen to what they're saying to the people who work with and for them. Check for quality. If it's absent, then getting them to shut-up is better than allowing them to bore others to tears while destroying their own credibility and damaging the organizational culture.

This is why preparation is so important. This is why laziness never pays, it always costs. Prepare and plan your communications. It doesn't take long. Know what it is you aim to achieve, consider who you're communicating with, choose the right channel, and then make sure you get the message across and get them to confirm that they heard what you said and understand precisely the meaning you intended.

Champion Clarity

It is crucial that you stamp out ambiguity where possible. Remember what we are talking about here: communication – something you'll spend eighty percent or more of your time sending, receiving, interpreting, and acting upon.

Telling someone, "You need to do a better job" is totally devoid of clarity. In fact, as a communication it's only use is to alienate the employee and make him feel uncomfortable. "You need to up your sales", or, "You need to work on your personal appearance" are all equally useless too. The danger here is that the person will either try nothing or come up with a solution on their own that does not match what you had in mind. But then again, how are they to know what you had on your mind if you never told them? Speak sentences like these and blame *will* migrate to *you*.

"I think you could do a better job if you put more upfront preparation and research into your projects and then ran a few ideas by your colleagues for some constructive criticism and input". Now *that* sentence adds clarity to your wish that this guy would do a better job.

"I think you should aim to sell one item per hour every hour from now on. Doing this will increase your daily average from six to eight and get you right back on track". *That* sentence adds some clarity to your wish that this guy would sell more.

"I want you to shower every morning without fail, iron your shirt and polish your shoes everyday before coming to work". That sentence adds so much more clarity to your wish that the guy work on his personal appearance.

From the other direction, ask questions of people if you suspect you don't fully understand what *they* are trying to communicate to you. Repeat back to them what you heard and encourage them to correct you if you're wrong. A lack of clarity is as bad as no communication at all. Make sure you create an atmosphere in which people feel safe communicating clearly, asking questions, restating things, correcting people they are talking to. If you don't, you'll spend far too much time managing the consequences of your own failure to champion clarity.

Working the Boards

We looked at this briefly in chapter 3.

You should refuse to talk to people if the room has nothing to write on for all to see. I immediately become suspicious if executives take me to a meeting in a room that has no white boards, no blank flip charts to write on, and the like; sitting around with individual hi-tech gadgets is no substitute!

Remember, there is no guarantee that what you say is what others hear. We all interpret communications in different ways for different reasons. Go back to what we said on the factors that influence constituency behavior; a person's mood will alter how she hears something. Her loyalty, temperament, history with the business, the rumors she's been hearing – and more – are all silently at work in her subconscious; her internal dialogue could be roaring varying emotions – fear, anger, sadness - resulting in her not really getting what you are trying to communicate.

Posting boards in a room and working them effectively enables you to ensure that your message is getting across. Diagrams, arrows, all aid the human brain in picturing precisely what is going on and seeing the links. Working the boards brings focus, prevents minds from wandering off, and – as we saw earlier – enables you to sideline the tangents for later attention thereby enabling you to stay on point and get things finished. In other words, lead your meetings; manage the input from others; manage all the suggestions coming to you - working the boards enables you to do precisely that.

Listening to Employees

We also touched upon this earlier in chapter 3.

Don't ever think that just because your employees aren't talking to you they aren't talking to *some*one. External web blogs, bitching to the four Constituencies around them – if they're not happy they *will* let *someone* know. What if it's your customers or clients?

Not listening to the people around you at work can warp the psychological contract against the organization and turn talented people into rocks to be dragged.

Your refusal to interact with them on a personal level *is* a communication: it's communicating things you'd rather not if only you could see the real cost of such behavior. Employees move from a, "If I work hard I'll be appreciated and rewarded," mentality to a, "They don't give a damn so why bother?" attitude.

This is why you will often hear that truly effective communication is a two-way street. It's not just about you talking and them listening – it must happen the other way around too. There must be interaction. There must be openness. There must be a lack of fear and a lack of threat of reprisal. There is collaboration in communication. And – most importantly – there must be the presence of sufficient ego-strength and a willingness to hear the unpleasant things and not just the glory items; if nobody can safely point out that the Emperor (that would be you!) is wearing no clothes, how suitable can your organizational culture ever become?!

Most of us were never taught how to get to the point or say what we really mean. It takes practice to fine tune the ability to dip into the maelstrom of thoughts whirling around inside your head and pluck out an insightful to-the-point comment. It's not easy to brush off the emotion and deliver the pure facts. Again, your job when leading is to guide and teach. Use the boards on the wall if necessary. Teach employees *how* to tell you what they need to tell you.

Plug into the grapevine every once in a while. Keep your finger on the pulse. What are people bitching about? Who's spreading the latest stuff around? Might you be able to use those people – with or without their knowledge – later for something really important? What's the rumor mill spinning this week? Remember, just because you know that what's going around is nonsense does not mean dismissing it as unimportant will not see it do some serious harm. As a manager, you're also there to manage the nonsense and the downright daft: these things can do some *real* damage if left ignored.

Remember that the whole point of leading and managing properly is this: you make *your* life easier, *your* career go farther... Listening to employees helps you cover your own ass too. Those sitting around you on the executive team may have been there too long. Sometimes people rely too heavily on reports, aggregated figures, statistics, metrics. These things don't always tell you the crucial synergies at play and how to manipulate them to the organization's advantage. Don't tell the people around you to lead or manage by walking around and then not do it yourself. Imagine how much more powerful and informed you'll be if a manager tells you that some workers said x, and you yourself could reply by saying, "Yes, I spoke to those workers myself this morning but that's not what I read into what they were saying"!

Get the Right Take on Feedback

I simply do not understand managers or business owners who only ever give feedback in once-per-year sessions. Talk about making life difficult for yourself! Why on earth would you suffer for an entire year waiting for that one conversation?

Feedback, interaction, and communication should be two-way, ongoing, and constant. It should be of value and worth, not just mindless chatter for the sake of it.

Feedback needs to occur ASAP – as close to the event at issue as possible. If someone is not performing as they should, or they miss a deadline or target, be fast in pointing this out to them. In fact, with ongoing feedback and two-way communication you should be able to get to a person *before* the deadline is missed.

Always be one-hundred percent certain of your facts. Go check things out for yourself. Set yourself up for success by giving clear and concise instructions with steps to be followed in case of unforeseen occurrences, i.e. tackle the Blame Shifters[52] upfront. If necessary, go witness behavior for yourself, get the figures, try the product, listen to the calls with clients - whatever. And remember, sometimes politics is at work or the person snitching is experiencing a "straw that broke the camel's back" episode.

Feedback, to be effective, must be relevant, timely, unambiguous, and it must go to the right person through the most appropriate communication channel. Where necessary, give feedback and then invite some brief comments to ensure clarity and understanding.

Champion Open, Fair, and Transparent Decision-Making Processes

In organizational life, you're rarely looking for a one hundred percent majority agreeing with you: consensus is very often the order of the day.

You'll never win everyone to your side. But if the way in which you make decisions is consistent, fair, open to input from others, and transparent in how the decisions are made, then even those disagreeing with you will very often go along: consensus. They'll think to themselves, "I don't agree with this but I know he listened to me and I can see why he reached the decision he did".

---

[52] The concept of "Blame Shifters" is discussed more fully later in Chapter 9.

Time and time again, research has shown that an open, fair, and transparent decision-making process helps to bring people along even if they disagree with the final decision. Think of the alternative: you pop an idea through a slit in the boardroom door where a group of people you hardly ever see reaches a decision using some secretive set of criteria. Rather than consensus, such a system would be more likely to generate simmering anger, revolt, and hatred.

So it's not always about unanimity. It's about consensus built upon a foundation of trust engendered by transparent and fair decision-making processes that are not based upon rank or special interests. You want people around you to always know that you seek, welcome, and value their opinion; but they must also know that your decisions will always be based:

- On facts;
- On Research;
- In line with the right vision and strategy;
- On the way you want to shape the organizational culture.

Transparent and consistent decision making criteria foster trust, buy-in, and commitment. Never forget your own personalized Leadership Brand; consistency and transparency should be huge parts of this – people must know what they can *always* expect from you.

The Dangers of Insisting Upon *Too Much* Initiative

I'm weary of managers who tell their employees never to come to them with a problem unless they've got two or three possible solutions to suggest. That way – or so the logic goes – most of them solve problems all by themselves. But what if they can't think of a solution and this results in them not approaching you sooner?

You can't have people afraid to say anything, sitting watching the world fall apart while they try to come up with solutions all by themselves, or afraid that admitting an error is a sign of weakness on their part and a career-damaging move – communication is essential: policies or organizational cultures that prevent or inhibit it make little sense.

Self-Fulfilling Prophecy

Very often, if you keep telling yourself you're going to fail – you'll fail. If we expect that an employee is going to foul something up, our own behavior – hovering round and watching them more closely than usual – can cause this to happen: self-fulfilling prophecy and the Set-Up-To-Fail Syndrome. [53]

In management, the trick is to make sure you bring about good consequences rather than bad. Here, we can link back to what we said earlier about the Pygmalion Effect: if we start from a position of seeing peoples good qualities and seek to catch them doing something right, then our behaviors as managers stand a far greater chance of brining about the type of self-fulfilling prophecy that benefits the business. As Von Goethe has stated:

> Treat a man as he appears to be and you make him worse. But treat a man as if he already were what he potentially could be, and you make him what he should be.

Over time, *your* behavior when leading and managing has a very direct impact on how employees view themselves and their abilities. This is all part of our collaborative mutual

---

[53] Manzoni et al (2002).

interdependence idea: if I view you favorably, listen to you, guide you - you become a better employee in the long-term. I depend on you to get the job done and you depend on me to get out of your way.

Think of it from the other direction. I don't trust you as far as I could throw you. I micromanage everything you do because I'm certain you're going to foul something up and I tell you this regularly too. Now we have the reverse of the Pygmalion Effect – the Golem Effect. Now it seems I'm doing my best to bring about learned helplessness in you and everyone around you. In the long-run, you become paralyzed by fear, afraid to do anything in case you *do* get it wrong. You look to me for everything. In short, I end up doing everyone's job for them – my poor Choices cause me to increase the Demands made of me and the Constraints under which we must all operate.

Everything we are seeing here goes straight to the heart of why an ability to manage your full communications repertoire – and take time to understand and interpret the repertoires of those around you – is a key skill for effective leadership. Get the communications wrong, and you're in *big* trouble!

Call Them Out

If you think someone's got a problem with you, ask them – call them out. If someone seems unsure, a little confused, or not in agreement – call them out. If they're wavering on putting money in, coming onboard – whatever – call them out. You need to know what's going on, deal with it, or move to the next interested party.

Don't let conflict fester. Your fear or lack of energy in dealing with it can only come back to haunt you later as people stop talking to each other, start bitching, sour the atmosphere - and more.

Get people to make decisions. You're running a business. You can't sit around all day, all week, all year weighing the pros and cons. You've hired these people and pay them good money, so call them out – get them to nail their colors to the mast.

If you don't force people to say what you need to hear ("need" as opposed to "want" to hear) you could spend months working on something with people who intended pulling out toward the end all along. Call them out! Get them to tell you what they're thinking, what they're afraid of, what they're worried about. When you hear these things, you can move to reassure them before real lasting doubt sets in. You can tailor your sales pitches, your solutions, your approaches, and your language to suit *when* you *know* what's going on – and you can only know what's going on by calling them out.

Some Final Thoughts

Don't ever ignore communication or feel too busy to attend to it: *everything* stands or falls on communication issues.

Always strive to determine the right channel for the right person in the given context: unusual messages through usual channels won't stand out.

Use whiteboards or screens or flipcharts – whatever – to manage meetings, off-subject items, peoples' understanding: work the boards.

Remember, in today's world *too much* communication is the problem, *not* too little – quality is often lacking.

Insist upon clarity at *all* times: of yourself and from others. You are too busy to keep revisiting the same issues numerous times unnecessarily.

If in doubt call them out! Get things out into the open and deal with them.

Prepare and plan your communications; it doesn't take long. Know what it is you aim to achieve, consider who you're communicating with, choose the right channel, and then make sure you get the message across and get them to confirm that they understood what you intended in the way you intended

Don't wait for communication to come to you. Go investigate for yourself. Walk around, look, listen, interact; Discover problems before they even arise.

Chapter 6
Train Them

Everything we have covered so far goes to training - albeit in a subtle way without causing much resistance.

Some workers just don't want a promotion, or extra responsibility, or a big scary challenge, even if they are the best in the organization at what they do and natural candidates for promotion. Training these people for extra responsibilities would be a waste of time and resources (training as opposed to developing – everyone should improve on the self-development front to enable them interact and engage to the point where their skills and abilities are utilized to their full potential). And yet, on paper they look like perfect successors: personnel files *can* present false truths. With training, there are only two key points to remember:

- Your attitude/approach determines whether or not training is a benefit or a cost;
- Always put the time and effort in up-front to ensure a well considered approach is taken.

Training Only Costs If You Do It Wrong

If people don't need training, they don't need training - it's about as simple as that. It all depends on the work they do and whether updates, new methods, are required. Different industries develop at different speeds.

I see no reason why training should cost a fortune. If you're leading and managing – engaging with others - by walking around, getting people to come to you with their ideas, their feedback, their solutions, things they're hearing, then you can spread this around as managed knowledge. Interacting with people on a regular basis *is* a form of training and development for them because you're getting them to think, to analyze, to try new things.

The everyday workplace is full of people half-assing things, who don't know how to type on a keyboard, don't know how to use their computers to the best of their ability - lots of people can't do lots of things. Interact with people and you'll soon find out what they can and cannot do.

You'll know from the work environment in your organization whether or not people need to train at their desk or offsite. Is it too noisy? Are there too many distractions? Is the layout not conducive to training? Walk around observing with these things in mind and you'll reach a decision fairly quickly.

Look into who's delivering the training too. Go watch from the back for a while. Are they any good? We've all come across teachers and professors who couldn't teach if their lives depended on it, so don't assume that professional trainers are top notch. It's *your* money[54], so go find out what you're paying for.

---

[54] Not your personal money, of course, but money for which you are ultimately answerable. You'd be amazed how many business owners forget it's not *their* personal money!

And always go back to check up on what it is people are supposed to have been trained to do. Can they actually do what they are now certified to do? This is your return on investment – measure it. Make sure you got value for money, value for time, value for distraction from daily tasks and didn't get ripped off. Make sure people paid attention, listened, tried their best, and are now using their new knowledge. Remember, training is a cost or investment depending upon *your* behavior and attitude.

I worked for a company once that decided to send everyone for computer training. So off we went – those of us who didn't opt out that is. And here's the kicker: most who went already knew how to use the computers; it was a nice few days off. But those who opted out? You guessed it - they were the ones who didn't know how to use the computers properly. Then we all came back and life continued on.

Spot all the mistakes? They sent the wrong people, allowed the ones needing training to stay, paid for it all, and then didn't check back later to see whether the overall base standard of computer literacy had increased. What a waste of time and money. Managers who do such things should not be running anything.

Push Beyond "Job Required" Training

When you opt for short-sighted approaches you limit your ability to maneuver. If anyone else calls in sick, quits the company, gets promoted, or is fired, the only person who can step in is someone on their level or who works right next to them. Your training creates drones, blocks creativity, and can warp the psychological contract against the organization. Remember, teams with higher diversity often outperform smarter teams.

But imagine if all training was cross-functional and multi-level in nature. By this I mean designing training such that it incorporates insights into all the different departments and how managers on different levels have to deal with various issues. Seem like a waste of time and money? That's because, like most managers, you're looking at the *visible* costs but missing the *invisible benefits*.

If I show a bank teller how to use the new computer system and then show the kind of reports it generates, how each level of management then uses those reports and all the steps involved in all the other departments in the bank, then the employee starts to gain a better appreciation for what they do. They can see how doing or not doing something impacts people they rarely meet. They can understand how easily conflict can arise for seemingly irrelevant oversights. Often, they can even tell you why what you're doing is inefficient and how it ought to be done better.

"Why does the accounting department always ask for this stupid stuff? – it takes so long to prepare and is useless!" or, "Why can't I increase the reserve on an insurance file now instead of waiting until next Monday?" are the type of comments you'll hear when people have no insights into what managers need, why they need it, and what it all means. When this happens, you've got major disconnects – silos operating in ignorance of each others' needs and grating against each other rather than creating synergies to bring about efficiency, productivity, shared knowledge, and more. This kind of thing points straight to an absence of training that is cross-functional and multi-level in nature; it may also suggest inefficient processes.

Multi-functional, multi-level training enables you spot future candidates for promotion. It lets you see talents in people that they may not otherwise get an opportunity to show. Do you have any big-picture-seeing people stuck in the lower ranks? Do you have some people who can see all the links and join all the dots better than others? You would be amazed just how many personal assistants better understand the politics and how the organization works than the executives they trail behind day after day.

This broader approach to training, to induction, to development, to conversations – don't just use it in training - reduces conflict through affording people insights into what everyone else does and why they do it. It increases job rotation potential which in turn creates more versatile employees and a more nimble organization. Less supervision is required for people who know what they're doing even when moved from department to department, site to site. This in turn broadens your pool of potential promotion candidates: you could well be creating the trail blazers of tomorrow by using this approach. This aids in your succession planning. It builds commitment to the organization in employees, it ups their interest levels, and aids in motivating them through cutting down on boredom, giving them new challenges, and thereby reducing demands for pay raises. It allows them to use some of the creativity they might otherwise be storing up for off the job activities. And it enables you to up the diversity factor by mixing people in with others they haven't worked with before. Never forget: only about one in every ten people has all the required skills for truly effective leadership; many of these one-in-tens are not even in leadership positions!

Teach Them How to Constantly Reassess[55]

If your senior executives, managers, team leaders, supervisors – and all the others in charge of people – are incapable of constantly reassessing, then life becomes so much harder for the organization or business as a whole; you can't have a ship full of Brilliant Dullards![56]

Take a look at the Constantly Reassess Model below and follow the boxes from left to right as I move through the following short paragraphs:

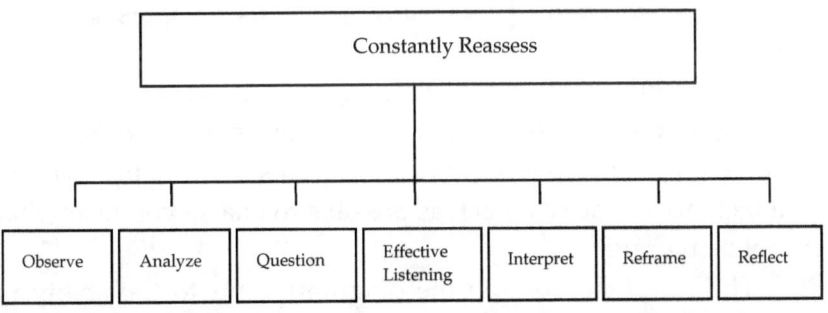

© 2008 Colm McCormack

Observation is absolutely essential for both effective leadership and management. If any of your team seems incapable of properly observing all that is going on around them, you have problems. Nobody should ever be "too busy" to observe. Far too many executives and managers look but don't see.

The key analytical ability when interacting with people is the ability to analyze words, expression, body language –

---

[55] For a detailed discussion on the concept of Constantly Reassess, see book 1 of this series: *The 'YOU' Factor: If You Cannot Manage Yourself, You Cannot Manage Others -* McCormack (2008), chapter 2.
[56] Discussed earlier in Chapter 2.

people! This takes time, practice, patience, experimentation – dedicated and focused experience.

There is an art to asking questions. Each member of your team needs to develop the ability to ask questions that get you the information you require without alienating everyone along the way. Too many managers run with the information they receive rather than pausing and asking questions about it.

The next box in the diagram points to the need to develop an ability to listen effectively. Each member in your team needs to be an investigator when asking questions. They need to get beyond the words to what is really going on or what is not being said.

An ability to interpret what they are hearing, seeing and sensing as they listen in an effective way is the next key skill along the road to Constantly Reassess. This is why I urge you to interact face-to-face as much as possible to enable you hear what is not being said.

The next box along in the diagram points to the ability to reframe. This requires maturity, ego strength, and a trained mind. Interpretation and reframing are not necessarily the same things. Interpretation can be said to be an exercise in looking for a true pattern or meaning whereas reframing can be described as finding the most useful way of understanding that pattern or meaning.

The final box is the ability to reflect. If you don't reflect you don't learn; it's about as simple as that. It takes me longer to read a book than it should simply because I spend a lot of time looking up from the text and staring off into space. I'm reflecting – thinking of a time when something did or did not apply, did or did not make sense. An experience only becomes an experience when you look back and think about it. That's why so many teams debrief. They chat about how a meeting went, how they think the sales pitch went, how an interview or intervention or planning session went. Only by looking back with calm can you learn the lessons of a storm.

Take just these seven skills – and only these seven – make sure that you and each member of your team are strong in them. Constantly Reassess is a key skill that *must not* go undeveloped in those who seek to lead and manage people. Its absence explains so many of the strategic and human missteps we read about year in and year out.

Teach Them to Experiment

An ability and a willingness to experiment are crucial in the worlds of business and management. Without experimenting, you never know just how far you can go. You won't always set your products and services at the right prices. Occasionally, you *will* hire or promote or fire the wrong people.

Experimentation enables you to determine whether or not you are correct in your interpretation of what you are seeing. You can't watch a person go nuts when asked to do something and then conclude they always go nuts every time they're asked to do something. Instead, you would come back the next day and the next week and ask them to do something: you'd experiment to test your conclusions.

Large retailers do the same week-in and week-out. They change prices, change offers, release and then discontinue coupons: they *experiment*! On the internet, they track clicks and click-throughs and time of day and number of hits and mix it all around: ongoing, never-ending experimentation aimed at learning and creating meaningful value.

If you can't get your team and those working with you to experiment, you won't go far. In fact, in certain industries you'll become extinct, and fast. The problem is we spend far too much time sitting around talking. I'm a big believer in the "good enough" attitude to business: you can't foresee or plan for every event without falling into paralysis-by-analysis so get things to "good enough" and then hit the road fine-tuning as you go.

Experimenting often trumps planning because you move from the abstract to the tried and tested. If carried out intelligently – if *managed* properly – experimenting can limit long-term risks and often help avoid disaster altogether.

Companies don't just flood the market with new products: they test them in isolated cities first. They get marketing companies to perform taste tests, to compile questionnaires for the public – they experiment.

Use a More Rounded Approach

I am a great believer in error-based training. By this I mean showing people all the mistakes any given company made and allowing the employees make their own suggestions as to what might have been done differently. And this is important. In today's time-pressured world, everyone wants the quick and easy solution. They all want the case studies showing how Wal-Mart or McDonalds or South West Airlines or Starbucks rose quickly to become giants. They want the "how-to" versions – the success stories.

But people learn so much more and become so much more creative in their thinking when presented with the companies that failed. Research has repeatedly shown that error-based training enables people to retain the lessons longer, to make more creative suggestions. So, we need to start mixing what we learn from Positive Deviants with the Error-Based teaching style to ensure the right lessons are learned in the right way and retained by the learners.

I also believe in Immersion. Swamp the person with nothing but what you are teaching or training them to do for a prolonged period until they become proficient at it. We see this with people trying to learn languages: their rate of proficiency increases dramatically when dropped into a country where that language is the first language. It's the same with work. I could spend days telling you how to make all the various Starbucks coffee offerings, but you'll learn so much more and far more quickly if I immerse you in the topic by making you work at the Starbucks counter for three or four days.

Remember all of this when training people. Don't just paint the rosy picture: show them where others have failed at the same thing and let them discuss alternatives. Don't just spend a few hours a week: immerse them totally for an extended period of time to avoid having to constantly revisit the topics later at increasing expense to the organization.

Get the basics right; lay a good foundation - *manage* the training and you'll get far better results *every* time.

Portfolio and Job Rotation

I remember asking the General Manager of a company I worked at to move me to another department before I died of boredom. I also wanted to learn more. I'll never forget his response: "*I wish I could. I'd love to move everyone around to give them a flavor for everything we do here. But I can't*". I didn't bother to ask why. Let's face it – if the top guy can't do something (or thinks he can't) what's the point?!

I subsequently left the company shortly after that conversation. Years later, I came to America and stayed for over a year on minimum wage simply because they kept training me in new parts of the business and moving me around regularly. Can you see the point I'm getting at here? Money is only *one* part of the overall motivational mix. I was earning good money with that General Manager who couldn't move me around yet I stayed part-time on minimum wage with another General Manager who kept me mobile, kept me learning, and kept me developing.

There are a number of points to take from this story. First; if you're into low-cost and cost-cutting, this story should leap off the page at you: keep people interested and they might stop bitching about wanting a pay raise!

Second; good workers with enthusiasm can walk away if you fail to hold their interest.

Third; a refusal to move people around can constitute standing in their way. If people are looking to take on more thereby making themselves more valuable to you, why would you ever stand in their way? Remember, the better each person on your team is, the better *you* will look.

Fourth; moving people around aids with succession planning, increases organizational flexibility, and smoothes out any ripples caused by illness or people leaving.

Fifth; you should conduct a skills audit of your employees on a regular basis. Do it early and then watch how more and more people gain more and more skills as you move them around.

Sixth; any career planning you decide to do becomes more informed. You'll get to see who the specialists are and who the generalists are. You'll get to see who's good at what.

Seven; you can move away from academic skills and introduce real on-the-job experience – experience that is multi-functional, multi-level, and multi-faceted. You can also ensure that an individual employee's experience is not all based in one area.

Eighth; moving a person around can also aid in disposing of them. Some people simply cause trouble. Moving them can isolate them. If a huge portion of their power comes from their expertise in one thing, move them!

But bear in mind a number of important caveats when discussing the rotation of employees. First, being good at something can often hold a person back or cause their manager to hold them in that position. There is a sense of security in sticking with what we're good at or keeping a person good at a thing doing that thing forever; this works for Brilliant Dullards (we covered this earlier) but not for others who become tired or bored due to lack of career progression.

A second point to bear in mind is that some people are simply better at some things than others.

A third and final point many business and management authors overlook is the *cost* of employee rotation. Think about it: when anyone tries something new they're slow at it and unsure. So it takes time to come fully up to speed. All *you* have to decide is whether or not this short drop in performance is far exceeded by the long-term benefits rotation will bring. Just never lose sight of this: how dumb must you be to say No to an energetic, enthusiastic worker who comes to you proactively offering to take on extra work and responsibilities?!

Giving Feedback – Some Simple Basics

Take careful note of what you are aiming for: people willing to talk about and hear about their mistakes from others. *You* need to lead and manage everyone into this position and then manage each session where all of this occurs. You also need to show people how to give feedback otherwise it will become a mudslinging contest where more harm is done than good. Some simple rules for giving feedback would include:

- No back stabbing;
- No complaining;
- No alienating everyone around you;

- No attacking the dignity of the person under scrutiny;
- No aggression.

This process takes us back to Positive Productive Blame mentioned in Book One.[57] When people make a mistake but learn from it and are not punished - because it was an intelligent mistake - then the blame leads to a productive experience that becomes positive due to exploring it, learning from it, and sharing the lessons with the rest of the organization.

When developing people in their career, they should be aware that feedback will not always be wonderful or what they wanted or what they expected. Executives, managers, employees - all must be able to give and, more importantly, receive feedback. This takes practice in an environment and culture of trust where they feel secure and know they will not be punished for offering feedback or for the feedback directed at them.

Teach Them the Defense Mechanisms

A huge part of getting people to try something new is first explaining to them the ways in which a person in their position typically reacts. And it's the same, for example, when putting people into new teams: you should teach them the various stages a new team goes through before becoming truly effective.

If you want to get people to give and receive feedback, you need to teach them how to give and how to receive. Let's deal with receiving feedback first. For this, they really should be aware of the various defense mechanisms their minds will call into play.

The most obvious in the business and management world is defensiveness. We all know this from confronting non-

---

[57] See: McCormack (2008) chapter 3.

performers or when confronted ourselves. Sometimes it occurs simply because we spend so long working on something that we rush to defend it when others start poking at it and asking questions.

Next; denial. "That wasn't me", "It's not *my* fault", – these are the type of lines managers get everyday.

Regression is another defense mechanism. It refers to behaving like a child. We've all seen temper tantrums and door slamming, people storming off or bashing their computers.

Next; rationalization. It takes courage to admit when we are wrong. Rationalization refers to covering your own ass when things get fouled up.

Projection refers to projecting feelings and motives onto others in order to protect your own ego.

Finally, fixation. Inflexibility of attitude and approach is what we are getting at here. We all fall victim to this one and exercise this particular defense ourselves on occasion.

There are, of course, more defense mechanisms than I have listed here, but these are the main ones to be alert for in organizations. If you can explain these to the people working with you, give examples, list them on the board and then point to them when you think someone is using one, you will teach a lot and enable greater progress.

Teach Them the Steps to *In*effectiveness

Showing people the steps toward ineffectiveness conjures up the benefits of Error-Based learning: they start to see the proper way of doing things thereby exhibiting less resistance to you showing them the right way to do things. Take a look at the following table from Book one:

Proceed	Pausing rarely happens in any meaningful way
One-Dimensional View	Positions not properly considered, or only their own and those of a limited few others are considered
Weakened Perspective	Theirs only (and perhaps the perspective of only one or two others) is considered
No Prevention	A bad start is less likely to prevent them avoiding making the wrong Choices thereby increasing/worsening the Demands made of them and increasing/worsening the Constraints under which they must operate
Fall off in Positivity	Greater likelihood that your perspective and attitude will be unchanged (at best) or negative (at worst). Only dumb luck or chance can deliver meaningful results
Poor Preparation	Haphazard (if at all) or totally inadequate due to previous points listed above
Lack of Pro-Activity	Nothing in the first six steps here is Pro-active or Pre-emptive
Performance	Effective performance is now down to dumb luck or unwittingly correct moves. Proceeding without considering all the positions, without viewing the matter from multiple perspectives, and a lack of positive and suitable preparation is begging ineffective results
Negative Consistency	All of the steps here, if followed regularly, represent consistency: Negative Consistency[58]
Perpetuate	Perpetuating such a cycle will see them taking Action without a proper understanding of Context and devoid of Constantly Reassess (or reassessing the wrong things). This reaches out to negatively impact the Five Constituencies, sets unsuitable examples, warps the psychological contract and sees Blame Migrate to the person in question. It also sees them failing to return at the end of the cycle to the issue they began with. Instead, a multitude of differing problems are expected to present themselves all of which eclipse the original issue leaving it unresolved.

---

[58] In Book One, we split Consistency into three forms, one of which was Negative Consistency: consistently doing the wrong things and behaving in the wrong way. As mentioned in Book One, consistency gets such a bad rap these days, but viewing it as bad or out of date is totally incorrect. See: McCormack (2008) Chapter 4 for more in-depth discussion.

Paste this table to a board or on a large screen and let people mull over it for a while. Get them talking about each point and – if they're alert and willing to talk about it – watch them suggest alternatives. Demand reasons for the alternatives. You want to see how they're thinking. Then go back to book one in this series and compare what they've suggested to what I suggest the alternative – the steps to being truly effective – should be.

Taking this approach – a participative approach using error-based learning – is so much better and far more effective than simply ramming a how-to lecture down their throats.

Some Final Thoughts

Before diving into training, insist on carrying out a training needs analysis to ensure the right people are trained in the right things in the right way.

Insist on training containing portions that are multi-disciplinary and multi-level in focus to create greater organizational understanding and insight.

Teach the employees how to Constantly Reassess. Doing so makes the entire business more alert and adaptive.

Teach them:

- How to listen;
- How to come to the point;
- How to stay on point;
- How to give feedback;
- How to receive feedback;
- How to experiment intelligently.

All of these things help to build ego-strength, champion clarity, improve them as employees, and make your job easier.

Always be on the lookout for opportunities to rotate people into different functions or roles. Broaden people's skill bases and knowledge where possible to benefit the day-to-day running of the business and the future promotion/succession potential of the organization.

Always measure your Return-on-Investment for training. Was it worth the money? Are you better off after all the training? Has behavior changed for the better?

Nowhere is it stated that reframing must produce a positive and optimistic alternative. Business and management books seem to lean exclusively toward reframing in the positive. And there is good reason for this: it takes a trained and disciplined mind to see all choices and choose calmly from among them. But it would be remiss of me not to mention what I term "the darker side" of all the models, frameworks, and approaches I discuss in my books. As I warned previously in book 1, blind optimism is *not* what we are looking for here. The mature and effective manager considers an issue or person from all perspectives – good and bad. There are often times when reframing something in a poorer light can prevent you from making horrendous errors. Training people in the right way – you will recall "Reframe" was one of the seven boxes in the Constantly Reassess diagram – can aid here. Make sure those working with you can reframe in multiple directions: in the positive, in the negative, in the neutral, and in the unforeseen.

Chapter 7
Develop Them

The whole point of improving your ability to lead and manage is to better enable yourself get out of the way of the people you have appointed to do specific jobs: it's about as simple as that. Remember: when you switch to leadership mode, you are, in effect, working for *them*. As I have said and will continue to say – it never ceases to amaze me how many managers hire people to do a job and then seem to place as much in the way of getting that job done as possible; I see this kind of thing every day.

Make your own life easier over the medium- to long-term by front loading your efforts; engage with those around you to set the suitable example and enable them to replicate that suitable work behavior. Then, install reward systems to lock-in that behavior which, over time, becomes the new organizational culture.

Training – we looked at this in the previous chapter – can, over the long-term, see diminished returns if not accompanied by employee development. Teaching people set things is of limited value, but teaching them *how* to learn and how to be effective with their knowledge is vital. People who never learn how to learn will forever be at the mercy of misunderstood context, fads, changing trends, and herd mentality.

> Education is an admirable thing, but it is well to remember from time to time that nothing that is worth knowing can be taught.[59]

Drumming static skills into people is useless if those people are not instilled with the ability to reassess changing context and recognize when what they know is useless or wrong. Far too many managers automatically apply the same tired old solutions to new and evolving problems: they don't know *how* to learn. But the Constantly Reassess model with its seven boxes in the last chapter should aid here.

Change Your Perspective

Development of employees occurs on a daily basis if you're walking around interacting with them, pressing them for input, asking them to point out problems and asking them to suggest solutions; giving them feedback and soliciting feedback from them. What does *that* cost?

You should start to view your employees – especially those in charge of others – as depreciating assets. The only way to retain their value is to keep them up to speed. You cannot expect excellent people to come through the doors on day one and retain their shine forever.

Managers are usually all trained the same way and get promoted for excelling at doing a small number of things. But what got them to their current position could well be very different from what is required to get them and the organization to the next level. People become comfortable with what they have achieved and how they do things. Then they stop learning. They become creatures of habit, slaves to models and frameworks they've carried around in their heads for years, and start using the same old techniques in new situations; often,

---

[59] Oscar Wilde.

much to the frustration of new workers who have arrived from outside the organization and can see immediately the barriers such once brilliant managers now present to progress.

Remember; you are mingling with regular employees to get beyond the numbers and reports. If you find one team not exhibiting the desired approach, you only have one person to tackle: their manager. How many so-called "Leaders" listen only to their top team and remain clueless as a result?! Exactly: too many! Give every person in the organization a voice by getting out among them; pierce through the veil of your direct reports and go very often to the front lines to see and hear for yourself.

Must You Develop *Every* Employee?

Think about what a lot of authors, gurus, and professors out there have been advocating for some years now: let employees make decisions and manage themselves. This is a utopia that can only happen in small pockets for a number of reasons:

- Some employees don't want responsibility. They don't want promotion, hassle, or a hard life;
- Some employees come to work to socialize – and that's about it. It's a place to hang out with pals, to get away from the kids, or to make free phone calls and surf the web between long coffee breaks and lunches: work fulfills their social, security, and belonging needs;
- Some employees don't have the intelligence – actual or emotional – to participate in big important decision making and planning processes. A person can be smart but incapable of big-picture thinking. A person can be well-read but produce little, if any, original thoughts or insights;
- Some don't have the technical know-how;

- Some work for organizations where the management and organizational culture never seeks their opinion or punishes them when they offer it;
- And some workers don't have the communications skills or confidence to make worthwhile contributions.

Kids Get More Development than the Average Worker

It is only more difficult to develop adults in work than kids in school because employers generally do not have suitable long-term formalized employee development programs set out. The occasional training or weekend away white water rafting is about as considered as many programs ever get to be. But think about it – schools and colleges are systems. Work is often systemized but not toward development – only toward efficiency and productivity. Does your company have a four year long employee development program? That's the length of an undergraduate program. What about a twelve year long program? That's how long kids usually stay in school prior to even getting to undergraduate level. And yet, in work, we get the odd training session here and there, and then the rare personal development session once every few years.

> Raised through a childhood in which each new year brought novel opportunities, playing at ever more difficult levels of sports, growing physically, educated in a system of cleanly delineated grades – freshman, sophomore, junior, senior – many employees find themselves several years into their career wondering what happened to the momentum they used to enjoy...many workers are disappointed to discover there will be no dramatic difference between their experience as a 25-year-old employee and their experience as a 26-year-old.[60]

---

[60] Wagner et al (2006) p. 176.

Develop Them as People

You have no input into how employees were raised or lived their lives before they came to you, but boy will you have to deal with the consequences – good or bad!

Sometimes you're stuck with an employee: Laws can prevent you from ditching them; contracts can tie you in; your boss might like them or they may have connections higher up; the pool of people with the employee's particular skills may be small so there's no one else. And, of course, ditching someone and looking for a replacement takes time and money.

Start by talking to them regularly. You're not out to become their friend: you're running a business and making your own life easier. Call them out – if there's a problem or you think something's up, ask them. Be direct but not offensive. Be firm, but polite. This gets them used to the idea that confrontation is not bad; it's healthy if carried out in the right way. It also gets them used to the idea that conflict is productive so long as the dignity of the person is not attacked.

By showing that you're willing to come right out and say something, ask something, challenge something - and at the same time demonstrating you won't hang anyone for telling you the truth or for pushing back a little - you start to steer people into the type of behaviors needed to improve the organization.

If they're shy, ask them questions and get them to demonstrate their answers. If they're insecure, build them up. If they dither or never contribute anything, call them out – shut others up and get these people to make a decision or add something to the conversation. When they do, give a little nod to them as encouragement. And then don't let up; always demand their views, always ask what they think could be done better and why.

If they complain a lot, tell them. Let them know it's irritating, that it's dragging them down, that others get tired listening to it. Tell them you know they're better than that – give them a better image to live up to. If they have bad habits, point them out and show them how you think these habits get in their way. But always finish in the listening position. Ask them for their thoughts on what you've just said.

If a worker is always butting in, hogging the air time, ramming his point home at the expense of others, tell him. Manage him. Tell him to be quiet for a moment and then get the views of everyone else. Encourage healthy and meaningful discussion, debate, confrontation, and conflict.[61] Your job as a manager is to raise a topic and then manage how others run with it. It's not your job to raise a topic and then spend the entire meeting talking about it yourself. It's not *your* meeting just because you called it: it's *our* meeting!

You're there to listen, get input, assess peoples' depth of understanding and insight, to see what they have to offer, and – most importantly – to interject only when they go off topic or when someone is doing all the talking while others do none.

If you can change how someone thinks about something, or how they feel about it, or how they behave toward something, this can have a ripple effect across other fronts. We saw this in Book One when looking at the Greenberger and Padesky[62] approach for dealing with personal issues. They indicate five aspects to our life experiences:

- Our thoughts;
- Our moods;
- Our behaviors;
- Our physical reactions;
- And the environment in which we find ourselves.

---

[61] I strongly encourage you to explore DeBono's *Six Thinking Hats*, here.
[62] Greenberger et al (1995). Featured in book 1, see: *If You Cannot Manage Yourself, You Cannot Manage Others* - McCormack (2008) chapter 2.

A change in any one of these aspects can impact all of the others. If I can get you to change the way you <u>think</u> about a problem or issue then your <u>mood</u> in relation to it will change, your <u>behavior</u> will change, your <u>physical</u> <u>reactions</u> will change and the <u>environment</u> around you will change because of your new mood, perspective, and behavior.

When a new team is put together, I often insist at the very first get together that team members stand up and give a five minute talk about themselves. Speaking in public is consistently ranked as the biggest fear most people have. I want to see who can do this and how they perform: do they fidget/stutter/shift from foot to foot/walk aimlessly about/make or fail to make eye contact?

When they're comfortable presenting information to the group, I'll get them to take questions. Then I'll get them to come to another group and get them to present something and take questions. Slowly but surely, over a very short period of time, I move people who have rarely (if ever) given a public speech to being comfortable standing and taking questions from strangers. And it all brings about many benefits: it builds their confidence and instills focus; it builds ego strength; it takes them out of their comfort zone to bring about personal development; they learn to deal with criticism and the unknown together with seeing how to defend their ideas rather than themselves.

It may take you a few months before people are more open, more willing to contribute, but it *will* be worth the effort: flying solo is not something anyone seeking to lead or manage in an effective way can do for very long.

Start Building Their Ego Strength

A major point behind engaging with people by walking around is demonstrating to them that you will listen and not rush to punish those who speak out, or make suggestions, or try new ideas; it also gets *you* beyond reports to see and hear from the frontlines yourself. Part of this process is to move people to a point where they can talk openly about their own mistakes, what they might have done better, and more. When you get people doing that, you're on the road to increasing their ego strength.

Ego strength refers to your ability – or lack thereof – to maintain emotional stability and cope with stress. When referring to a person's ego getting in the way we are discussing a person's pride and their need to save face and protect their reputation. Underlying such behavior is the presence or lack of ego strength.

The old conventional wisdom that you should leave your ego at the door is wrong: you must not proceed through the door without sufficient ego strength.[63] If people didn't have big egos, a lot would never get done. Surgeons need big egos. So too do fighter pilots, business people, entrepreneurs and innovators. So, ego is not a bad thing: it can make the difference between going someplace and going nowhere. But it's the unbridled out of control *unmanaged* ego we need to worry about.

> My advice is yes, have a big ego, but do not be egotistical. A big ego is a positive thing.[64]

When employees can take feedback and constructive criticism from those around them, they become even better. They learn to analyze the results they got and what they did. They ask questions of those giving them feedback. They employ a more effective listening style to ensure they fully understand what people are suggesting to them. They learn to reframe the entire experience as a learning exercise and something to share

---

[63] For further discussion, see book 1 in this series: McCormack (2008) chapter 5.
[64] Trump (2007) p. 280.

with others to benefit everyone. And then they get to reflect upon the entire process later when they have some quiet time. Analyze, question, effectively listen, reframe, reflect – you should recognize these steps from the Constantly Reassess diagram we encountered earlier.

Champion Diversity

There is no truer adage than this: travel broadens the mind. And it's not just about going places: it's about sights, sounds, smells, cuisine, social norms and taboos – the way different people view and do things differently.

One of the great advantages to sending your kids on semesters abroad to Europe – and then allowing them to tour Europe during summer break – is they get to encounter so much diversity. Just experiencing these things broadens their way of thinking, their sense of humor, and so much more.

And it should be the same in the work setting. I prefer the internal makeup of a business to mirror its external surroundings as closely as possible. Remember, the more employees are alike – for example; all male, white, and over fifty – the less the group is a representation of the real world outside. I prefer to see the senior management team of any organization getting as close to a fifty-fifty split in male and female executives as possible with a healthy sprinkling of experience from other countries and industries. (An important qualification on this point of diversity: similar-*minded* teams have the ability to achieve the remarkable. You *never* want diversity of focus and energy and motivation!)

How is *your* organization made up? Is there much diversity? Do you need much? How do you decide such a thing? How do you define "diversity"?

Diversity is about employing people who have traveled, people who have worked abroad, people *from* abroad, people who have worked in different industries, and more.

Today, "diversity" has come to mean gender or skin color but such limited definitions are of little benefit to the business world. The old-fashioned all-white-male-over-fifty boardroom and executive team is not as old fashioned as you might think – just glance at the websites of major corporations today to confirm this. And this goes for the general body of employees too. But beware: if the general body of employees is more diverse than your senior team in experience, background – and all the other things I just mentioned – they may become unhappy pretty quickly because of the inflexibility of your senior team relative to the mindset of the employees.

> The diversity of any system determines its capacity to adapt...The risk in a fast-changing world is that a company becomes *overadapted* to a particular ecological niche...As change accelerates, investing in diversity is not a luxury; it's a survival strategy...Despite all the rhetoric to the contrary, companies often put more effort into training the diversity *out* of people, through programs that indoctrinate employees in the "one best way," than they do into bringing fresh ideas *into* the company.[65]

Never forget; diverse leadership teams outperform smarter teams, so reach for diversity!

Don't Tell – Ask!

"Ask" saves so much time, opens so many doors, and helps you get to the *real* point. But there's a second side to this wonderful little word: it enables you to teach and develop people around you.

When you tell someone how to do something or tell them what's wrong in any given situation, you're not enabling them

---

[65] Hamel (2007) p. 18.

to do a whole lot of thinking. You're simply spoon-feeding the answer to them probably because you don't have a lot of time or patience. But, as with so many things in life, when you front-load your efforts you generally save far more time on the backend.

Asking someone why they think something didn't work out, or why they think something went right or wrong, forces them to think. And you do this in a supportive and interested way too.

When you know the answer, ask anyway. Use your questions to guide the person through analyzing what has occurred and to assess their future potential. Ask them how they think things can be improved or how a success can be repeated. Ask them what they thought of your own suggestions and ideas – may as well benefit from the experience yourself and not have all the learning flowing in one direction only! With each point they give, ask them why. This has become known as the Socratic Approach. People learn far more when they think for themselves underpinned by the safety net of an advisor, mentor, or teacher who is supportive and who coaxes them along.

Get Them to Defend Their *Ideas*, NOT Themselves

Defensiveness is one of the major reasons managers derail. But there's nothing to say this is a problem to be stamped out in the managerial ranks alone. Kill off the defensiveness in all your workers and you'll increase the quality and success of communication in the organization.

You should already have been working to ensure that for meaningful and worthwhile constructive criticism to occur, no personal attacks are tolerated. That's the first stumbling block.

The second stumbling block occurs when people view an attack on their ideas or suggestions as attacks on them as a person. In many ways this is understandable. When you've worked and thought hard on a project, it becomes deeply personal.

You need to move people toward defending their *ideas* and *not* themselves. Here are some guidelines:

- Start Working the Boards: People are looking at the points up on the wall and *not* directly at the person who made them. This is a positive version of dehumanizing: take the person out of the equation and deal with his argument;
- Start Managing Communication: Don't allow anyone to make personal attacks. If they do, call them on it right there in front of everyone to show it will not be tolerated. Very often people don't realize when they've crossed from constructive criticism to personal attack;
- Start Managing Responses: If someone starts defending themselves rather than their ideas, call them on it. Again, do this in front of everyone to show that this is not how you want things to run and also to help the person recognize when they have strayed into focusing on themselves rather than the issue at hand;
- Emphasize the Points: Don't keep referring to something as "Tom's point". Instead, simply write it up on the boards and deal with it as a point with no personal connection to anyone.

A failure to get people debating and defending their *ideas* rather than themselves limits the potential of the organization: It stifles true creativity and flexibility; it brings about an unsuitable organizational culture; it blinds people to sensible alternatives. And in the end, blame for such results will migrate to the manager who refused to develop people away from such behaviors.

Get Them to Turn Problems into Verbs

Choice Theory is a branch of psychology that explains how people choose everything they do and everything they feel.[66] Under the theory, for example, people are not viewed as being depressed: they are viewed as depress-ing, i.e. they are deliberately choosing to feel depressed whether they realize or accept this or not.

> To be depressed or neurotic is passive. It happened to us; we are its victim, and we have no control over it...With verbs, you are not a victim of a mental illness; you are either the beneficiary of your own good choices or the victim of your own bad choices...A choice theory world is a tough, responsible world; you cannot use grammar to escape responsibility for what you are doing.[67]

Now let us take Choice Theory and apply it to people at work. Instead of "My career is stuck", or, "I'm stuck in this job", we can say that the correct view – or reframing it differently – would see us use the word "sticking", i.e. "Whether I realize it or not I am *sticking* here in this dead end job and haven't done enough to get myself out of it. Therefore, it's my choice and I am responsible for being where I am".

See the difference? Using external locus of control – allowing things and people *outside* of them as a person control their life - allows a person to blame, to continue sitting in their own unhappy circumstances, and to seek comfort in such an attitude thereby not having to do anything about it. But when we flick from the noun "stuck" to the verb "sticking", suddenly responsibility enters the fray. Now external locus of control exits and is replaced by internal locus of control; internal meaning the person himself is taking responsibility and attempting to take

---

[66] Choice Theory was created by psychiatrist William Glasser, M.D. See his book: Choice Theory: *A New Psychology of Personal Freedom*. Full details contained in bibliography at the back of this book.
[67] Glasser (1998) p. 77.

control of his circumstances. We have simply reframed the same situation to view it from another perspective.

This is something you need all of the people working with and for you to become good at: they need to be able to reframe along the lines of turning nouns that describe a situation into verbs. When you can get people doing this, creativity and flexibility arrive together with responsibility, problem-solving and solution finding. You switch out problem-oriented mindsets and replace them with solution-oriented ones. You avoid adopting short-term solutions (complaining and blaming) devoid of long-term focus (if you don't fix it things will stay the same).

So the next time someone complains "I'm going nowhere", you can think to yourself, "Boy, you said it! 'Go-ing' is right but that's a choice *you've* made". As we saw in book 1, negative information usually gives you the answer.[68] In the complaint, "nowhere" is the result but "I'm going" is the key – and that's the part that needs to change.

Seek Out and Destroy Negative Synergies

The idea of groups and teams is that they should produce more as units than if the individuals were working alone: one person plus one person should hopefully produce the results of three people or more. "Produce" here doesn't just refer to parts or products: it also refers to ideas, solutions, and more.

One of your jobs is to determine where this rule breaks down: do you have a group that is not creating the $1 + 1 = 3$ that you would expect?

---

[68] For more on how answers can be gleaned from complaints or stated problems, see: Pierce (2003).

There are a number of reasons why this failure to achieve synergies or, in extreme cases, why *negative* synergies (1 + 1 = 1 or zero or -1) can happen:

- Social Loafing: some people do less while others pick up the slack;
- Lack of Knowledge: people may not know how to do something or not know of a better way to do it;
- Lack of Clarity: delegation may have been poor and insufficient. People may not know precisely what is required of them and therefore have to make a lot of it up as they go;
- Learned Helplessness: a manager who insists on being involved in absolutely everything and always lurking over employee's shoulders can ultimately teach employees to become useless;
- Perception of Inequity: sometimes people – correctly or otherwise – form the view that others are not working as hard as they are or are getting paid more, or whatever. Whether or not such perceptions are logical or daft is rarely the issue: it's the consequent reactionary behavior to such perceptions that are the problem;[69]
- Incentive and Reward Systems: very often you will find that people are herded together as a group or team and yet they are still rewarded on an individual basis. This causes internal conflict and eventually you may expect that self-rewarding behavior will take precedence over what's best for the group or organization;
- Lack of Confrontation and Conflict: if you cannot confront another group or team member, how will you ever stop them engaging in social loafing? If there is no conflict, how

---

[69] For more detailed discussion on this point, see Book One: McCormack (2008) Chapter 4: *Dangerous Power of Perceptions*. That section touched upon Equity Theory of Motivation.

do you ensure ideas get thrashed out fully to ensure the best option is chosen?

- Just not a Team Player: some people simply don't like being in a group or team. Some people prefer to be loaners relying on themselves.

360-Degree Feedback

I dislike 360-degree feedback for two main reasons: *how* it is carried out and *who* it is that carries it out.

First; this form of feedback is often carried out in a non-face-to-face way. As unbelievable as it may sound, many companies carry this out online. Some managers feel they are simply too busy so they get employees to comment on each other through the in-house computer setup. Of course, before long, employees start protecting each other so the constructive criticism becomes mere compliment-giving in the expectation that if you scratch my back I'll scratch yours. Corporations usually also have limited budgets for review with some even secretly operating systems whereby x-amount of dollars will go by way of bonuses or pay increases irrespective of the *actual* performance.

My second concern is with the people who carry out 360-degree feedback sessions. Most are not trained properly and can cause more harm than good. Remember, business and management schools do not teach you how to read, manage, or interact with people in a meaningful way: these are all things you are assumed to have learned fully when growing up!

It is far too easy to read about how wonderful 360-degree feedback is and then launch half-assed into a similar setup in your own organization. Let me give you an example.

I stood at a distance in a large American retailer one time and listened to the employees chatting. Their manager had called them into a group in the middle of the store and asked them all to tell Jane what she was doing wrong in her job and how she might make small improvements to get herself up to speed. All the employees participated and Jane listened. When the conversation was finished, she thanked her colleagues, the manager thanked everyone for getting involved and indicated they would revisit Jane's performance in a few weeks. Sounds great, doesn't it?

Well, yes it is – *when* it works! If you or I tried replicating this we'd probably cause more harm than good. And here's why: we would try to mimic precisely what we saw. The huge missing part was the trust, commitment, buy-in, and feeling of safety that existed between Jane and her colleagues. They had obviously done this kind of thing many times before and Jane was only the latest of her colleagues to come under the spotlight. Try this out-of-the-blue in the average business and you'll probably start World War three!

But did you notice the other subtle element in the story: the lack of anonymity. Jane could see precisely who was making comments. She could listen right there and then. She didn't get some anonymous tick-box report card full of bad news. And the entire process was positively framed: the entire discussion was geared toward *helping* her in her career. It wasn't a kick-Jane-and-deny-her-a-bonus session.

If you decide to bring in 360-degree feedback as part of your employee development strategy, make sure you know how to manage it. Make sure people know how to give feedback. Ensure that the feedback is constructive and positively framed. Make sure the feedback is open and transparent: everyone should have the right to see and engage with those commenting if and when necessary.[70] Make sure people know how to receive feedback. Make sure definitive steps for progress are laid out and people are recognized for achieving the new goals set out

---

[70] A simple tenet of law and due process.

for them. Put simply: lead and manage the process and make sure it brings far more positives than negatives.

Allow Intelligent Failures and Intelligent Mistakes on a Small Scale

Whether it's children, peers, or employees: they *must* fail. They *must* make mistakes. If they always get an "A" and are always helped or always berated for getting things wrong, they'll crumble soon after emerging alone into the real world.

It's *your* job to manage such mistakes and failures. In a nutshell you must lead the development of your team. Managing how people make mistakes and how they fail enables you to ensure that such mistakes and failures occur on a small scale. The alternative is to sit back waiting for them to fail while at the same time putting the entire organization at risk.

You need to teach the people around you – at home and at work – to make intelligent mistakes, to fail intelligently, and to do all of these things on a small scale at first. If you don't, then blame for their inability to perform effectively *will* migrate back to you in time.

Finally, be careful to avoid creating needy and insecure employees. Instill them with the right attitude and tone. You want them saying, *"What did you think of that?"* or, *"How could I make it better?"* You don't want, *"Did I do okay (?) because I really tried..."*

Some Final Thoughts

Don't ever make the mistake of assuming maturity comes with age. Far too many managers and employees are pessimistic, overly defensive, incapable of listening to criticism, and more. You may not have had anything to do with how a person was raised but you'll sure have to deal with the consequences of how they were brought up and all their experiences to-date.

Make your own job easier by striving to develop people to the point where you start managing them *less* as they start managing themselves more.

Focus on building their ego-strength. You want to get them to the point where they talk openly and contribute regularly irrespective of whether or not the topic concerns a past failure on their part.

Insist on diversity in your management team: diversity of gender, race, age, experience, nationality. Everybody all seeing the world in the same way can only ever be a strength in a non-changing world. You *never* want diversity of minds.

Start using the power of "Ask". It's a short-cut to knowledge and it prompts people into creativity and learning for themselves.

Search for negative synergies. Simple corrections can deliver large improvements.

Go small scale on failures and mistakes. Contain the blast to ensure people learn without pulling the business down.

You have a choice: keep banging your head against the wall or start to slowly develop people toward becoming the workers they should be. You won't turn people into brilliant contributors and champions of the business in six-months: it's a journey, not a destination – an ongoing process. The rewards far outweigh the effort required and certainly far outweigh all the demands made of you and the constraints under which you'll have to manage if you choose *not* to develop them.

Chapter 8
Leverage Them

Everything you do must go through people at some point: it can't be avoided. Getting insights from all levels becomes more crucial as your organization or department or team expands and your ability to do everything and know everything diminishes. Remember: interacting and engaging is your way of working for them to ensure they in turn can deliver the desired results. Start as you mean to continue: interact with those around you and then leverage them to the maximum.

Leverage Their Creativity – and More

> The fact is, creativity is a human aptitude, like intelligence, musical ability, or eye-hand coordination....Make no mistake, your company is filled with video bloggers, mixers, hackers, mashers, tuners, and pod casters...Trust me, your employees are exercising their creativity *somewhere*, it just may not be at work.[71]

It never ceases to amaze me how even people at the very bottom of a standard blue or white collar-type business have insights into how a job or product or service can be improved. I've come across people who were quiet, sullen, looked like they

---

[71] Hamel (2007) p.52, 196.

couldn't string a coherent sentence together, but when I finally got them to start talking on something they knew about – the jobs they were doing everyday – they could tell me what was wrong and a better way to operate. Granted, the language was never anything you would want your mother to hear and I had to filter out a lot of moaning, bitterness, and other such things – but the insights were often things the managers had missed.

If you don't ask you probably won't be told. How many creative people are there in your business? I've come across lawyers who were better cooks than fully-qualified chefs and waiters who could design top-notch websites. If you don't interact with the people around you, you'll never hear of such things. And this can amount to an incorrect understanding on your part of any Knowledge Map you decide to draw. There's no point classifying knowledge according to who's doing what. Remember, half of us – or more – are in the wrong jobs. How many of your own people can do things but will never be asked to do those things because you have them operating under "job descriptions" that inhibit them? Maybe you don't need to outsource your website management, or your conference coordination, or your...whatever, at great expense – or maybe you *need* to outsource such things. If you don't know, go find out.

Employees are there to be leveraged. Plug into their creativity. Plug into their knowledge. Plug into their experiences. Plug into their networks. Ask questions and then listen to determine if they have anything worthwhile to contribute. It only takes a few extra minutes. Every once in a while, you *will* hear a little gem – a small detail – that *could* make a big difference.

Delegation and Why You Need to Use It

The best way to leverage people is to get them doing things that free up *your* time.

Delegation centers upon the idea of asking other people to do things while making them accountable for completing those tasks. But it is *not* about passing the buck: while they are *accountable* to you for not completing something, it is you who is ultimately *responsible* for the outcome. While it might be your job to do a thing and you delegate the doing of that thing to Joe but Joe screws it up, yes Joe is accountable to you and you can fire him; ultimately, however, the actual job and responsibility for getting it done was yours – it was *your* department or team or team member who dropped the ball - remember this! This is the double-edged aspect to a leadership role: you can pass work (delegate) to others, but you cannot worm your way out of. responsibility if, under your leadership, they fail to get the work done.

You delegate to untie your own hands; you delegate to make certain you yourself have the time required to complete the highest value tasks you yourself must achieve. You delegate to develop and train people, to get them ready for promotion. Delegation is a time management technique. It enables you to build trust in those you delegate to, it motivates others and, ultimately, it aids with succession planning and knowledge sharing.

Far too many managers try to hold on to everything out of fear nothing will be done properly. You should always delegate tasks that are better handled by others – unless of course you want to learn and master such tasks yourself. Make sure you delegate a mixed bag of desirable and not so desirable tasks; don't be the ass who dumps all the horrible stuff on others and thereby slowly erodes the organizational culture.

Make sure the person to whom you delegate has been trained, or is capable, and has access to the resources necessary to complete the task – get out of their way! Imagine telling someone to order $50,000 worth of food every week for a grocery department but never telling the accounting department that this person has authority to spend up to $50,000 per week, or never training the employee in how to determine what is needed, by when, and all the documentation required – it happens, believe me!

How to Delegate

Remember, when dealing with management and employees, *behavior* is the key. The Five R's - detailed below - aid you in locking-in desired behavior but, more importantly, it is *your* behavior as a manager when delegating that can move you toward or away from truly effective delegation. Clarity and communication are the order of the day for effective delegation.

- The First R is "Repeat". So you have described what you want the employee to do. They have said they will get to it. Now introduce certainty and the opportunity for clarification by getting the employee to repeat back to you what it is you want them to do. They should hit all the main points: "You want me to order all products for my department, each order to go out every Monday morning, I'm not to exceed $50,000 without first consulting you, but other than that or any other unforeseen problems I need only get back to you the last Friday morning of every month at 10am with brief progress reports". Hearing all of those main points lets you know that the person has the entirety of what is required of them;

- The second R is "Remind". After your brief meeting with them, send them an email or memo. Keep it short and cover the main points only. Don't introduce anything new or start discussing matters again. This email or memo serves as a reminder to both of you;

- The Third R is "Reinforce". Asking the employee to repeat the main points of the discussion back to you and sending the email or memo after the meeting reinforces each step in their mind and in yours too. The email or memo also serves as a reference for them to revisit if later confused and as a road map with guide posts for them to follow;

- The fourth R is "Record". You now have an agreed upon "official" record of what is to be done, who is to do it, the timelines. This avoids conflict and confusion in the future. With this, you have introduced clear Single Point Accountability for completion of the task. On the employee development front, this record is a good way for both you and the employee to track their progress and the increasing level of responsibilities they take on;

- And finally, the fifth R is "Return". Returning to the issue at agreed points along the timeline avoids you falling into either of two extremes - micro-managing or abdicating responsibility - and enables you to revisit the issue without offending, annoying, or intruding upon the person to whom you have delegated the task.

After a while if they're any good they'll start ending your brief encounters with "Okay, so it's up to me to order the merchandize subject to a limit of $50,000 per week. Above that figure and I've to give you a call. We'll meet every Friday at 10.30am for brief progress meetings. Okay, got it".

The Importance of Context to Delegation

You cannot delegate all the time. This is where the eight factors of context come into play. We touched upon these in Book One but they are worth repeating here[72]. Take a look at the following diagram together with accompanying table:

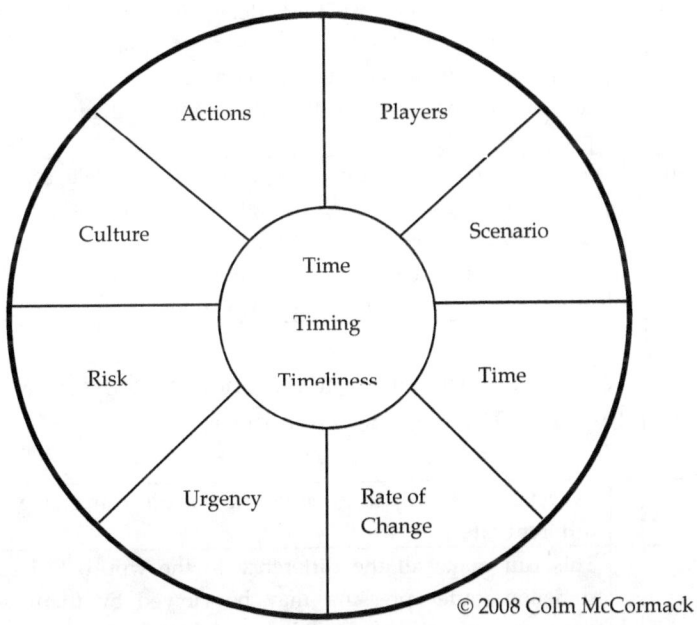

© 2008 Colm McCormack

Players	Who are you looking to delegate to? Are they trained for the task? Are they willing to perform it? Do they want extra responsibility or a quiet life?
Scenario	Is the business in trouble? Do you have the time to wait for a less experienced person to fumble through the task? Is there a major task coming *your* way thereby requiring you to offload some of your current Demands?
Time	Is it too late in the day, week, month, year? The concept of time is so important in management that it appears not just as a spoke in the wheel but also at the center of this diagram underpinning the entire model: it is both a factor and a support.

---

[72] See: McCormack (2008) chapter 7.

Rate of Change	Is the scenario static, evolving slowly, or changing rapidly?
Urgency	This matter may be urgent but is it highly important? If not, delegate it. If it is both urgent and highly important, keep a very close eye on its progress.
Risk	If you delegate this task and it goes wrong, how far beyond you and the person to whom it was delegated will the fallout spread? If you can contain the fallout, consider delegating it. If CNN end up parked out on the lawn, be very careful in your decision to delegate it, the terms of delegation, and your monitoring of its progress.
Culture	Is your organizational culture geared toward delegation? Might delegation cause surprise, shock, fear, suspicion? If it needs to be delegated, then delegate it and manage reactions accordingly.
Actions	Does the person spring into action? Do they stall? What do others do? These are all items to watch for.

All of these factors are underpinned at the center of the diagram by Time, Timing, and Timeliness:

Time	Everything is subject to time. All factors can change and at different rates.
Timing	This can make all the difference in the world. Delegating to someone under pressure may be viewed by them as being dumped on and having their workload increased unfairly. Delegating on a Friday evening as someone is about to leave for the weekend can ruin their time off.
Timeliness	There's no point delegating something if you do so too late. The same goes for delegating too early: you can distract people unnecessarily or forget about the task altogether.

Leverage Example-Setting

Monkey see – monkey Do! Behavior is a set of practiced, recognized, and accepted norms. If sitting around bitching about the economy, blaming everyone else, and shooting down suggested alternatives is the behavior regularly exhibited by the top dogs in your business, everyone else will do the same. Those who don't will either suffer in silence or go work for someone else.

And it works the other way too: taking responsibility, brainstorming, reframing problems as opportunities, and leaning toward solution-oriented mindsets and internal locus of control are all behaviors that can also be mimicked by others. Always remember that example-setting does not just flow from the top down: it spreads out, like ripples on a pond, from every person in every direction. Take a look at the diagram below that illustrates this:

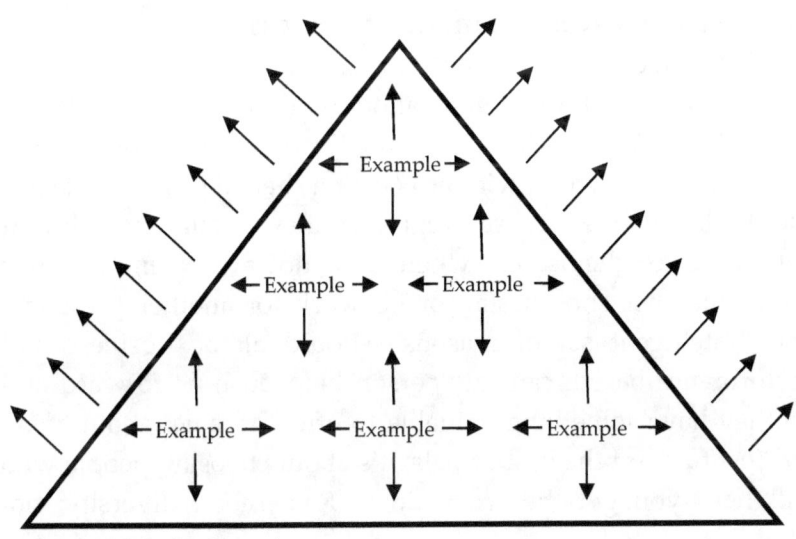

© 2008 Colm McCormack

As we can see, it doesn't matter what rank or position a person holds in an organization: their example-setting spreads out to everyone in all directions – not just downward to those beneath them in the chain or organizational chart – and out through all Five Constituencies.

Far too many managers leverage their example-setting in the wrong direction. They preach about frugality but then run up a giant expense account; they preach hard work but then stand around chatting all day with their peers. Their example-setting in such instances works against them: they leverage it to damage their credibility and, ultimately, the organization. Be very aware of this: preaching one thing but getting caught doing the other sets an unsuitable example, screams of hypocrisy, and creates an us-versus-them-type mentality. Make sure none of your managers are behaving this way, and make sure *you're* not either!

Enhance Group and Team Effectiveness[73]

Remember, organizations are social entities. Humans are social creatures. Both organizations and humans operate via networks. So long as there is an intelligent set of reasons behind it, I see nothing wrong with advocating that all groups or teams should be allowed to self-regulate: they should be allowed determine for themselves whether or not a new employee or group member should stay or go work for another company. The "intelligent set of reasons" should all be business and performance based: can this person help push us forward and do they have something valuable to offer? It is *not* about being the best fun and the best of pals: it's about choosing people who will help you get the work done. Remember: diversity; not clones!

Employees must be told that group cohesion and effectiveness do not kick-in automatically; some short-term disruption should be expected. The new member of the group may be unsure of what is expected of them, feel a little insecure, and therefore be slow to get up to speed. A power struggle may

---

[73] In strict technical terms there is of course a difference between a "group" and a "team" but we can deal with both at the same time so don't worry about intermingling the terms here.

develop as new knowledge and insights arrive in the form of a new member. This is all natural. Let it work itself out. If the group gets stuck fighting, then step in to help them along.

It's only when deep inter-personal conflicts develop that real problems arrive. Relationship or inter-personal problems – more often than not – are non-beneficial if not resolved quickly.

Allowing a group or team to self-regulate is a fantastic idea but highly dangerous and disruptive if not carefully qualified by the following criteria:

- The group or team must be fully educated on the theory of Group Think;
- They must be fully aware of the pros and cons of cloning themselves;[74]
- They must have been taught lessons in group/team cohesion, the various stages the new member and the group go through psychologically when thrown together thereby ensuring they don't misread natural occurrences and mistakenly cast a new member as a poor fit;
- They must have been moved some distance – both as individuals and as a group or team– along the road toward becoming Context Intelligent.[75]

Move Them from Co-Acting to *Inter*-Acting

It is important that you avoid what I term the "Co-Activity Syndrome".[76] A basketball team has players who interact with each other: they rely on each other for everything they do in a game. But in the workplace we often see people doing similar

---

[74] Mentioned in book 1, in particular see: *All the Right Principles in all the Wrong Places* - chapter 7 of McCormack (2008).

[75] See Book 1 in this series: McCormack (2008) chapter 7.

[76] See Book 1 in this series: McCormack (2008) chapter 9 for more comprehensive discussion on the Co-Activity Syndrome.

jobs yet going for hours on end without needing to help each other, or seek help, or coordinate with each other. This is known as "co-acting": they are acting beside each other but without much assisting or coordinating.

In truth, co-acting sees us miss out on vital synergies that might otherwise come about via *inter*acting. How many times have you gone to the office and left that evening without having had to interact with others to get things done? It happens quite a lot. And perhaps it should be no surprise to us since we pride ourselves as employees on our ability to work on our own initiative, our independence, our self-reliance. Now what we have are islands within the silos!

This is why people must get use to interacting, sharing ideas, openly confronting each other, dealing with conflict in a constructive way, brainstorming ideas, and more. It is for *you*, exercising leadership, to push them toward greater levels of comfort in these areas. Start with your top team first. If you can't get it right there, you're doomed. If some of the players won't get with the program, replace them. Get that top team right first, all loyal to the team and not their individual silos.

Then use engaging people by walking around, positive example setting – everything we've discussed so far – to get others on the right track. So long as people co-act you are missing out on achieving your full potential as an organization or department or team – which ever applies to you. You are missing out on learning opportunities, solution-finding opportunities, problem-solving discussions and debates. You must enable employees take best practices from other teams in the building or throughout the organization. Not doing so constitutes getting in their way, impacting negatively on trust, and warping the psychological contract. Get your organization firing on all cylinders: move employees from co-acting to *inter*-acting.

Get Them Training Each Other

If you think you understand something, try teaching it! It's only when you have to spend an hour or so talking about something in detail and teaching it to a room of people that you discover how well – or not – you know a thing. And this is important: teaching benefits *you* too since it reinforces the knowledge in your own brain. It's when people listening to you start asking questions that you really get to see if you know your stuff or not.

I quite simply don't understand managers who tell me they have an employee going to school at night – and then that's about as far as the conversation goes. Imagine having someone going to law school or business school but never plugging into what that employee is learning! Think about it - you can benefit so much more than one person: it cuts organizational costs and standing up to teach develops the person who has gone back to school even more. If the business has paid in any way for the employee to go back to school, then not leveraging this through passing on what they have learned becomes an even bigger mystery to me.

Instead of paying a small fortune for training and development, start leveraging your own employees. Here's a simple example. Get everyone in your company in sales to keep a diary for a few weeks. Get them to note what works for them and what doesn't, how the company aids them or gets in their way. Then gather them together and get them to swap diaries with the person next to them. They should read their colleagues diaries and then each make a brief presentation to the entire group of all the points – good and bad - they found useful and insightful. That way, after everyone in the group has presented, you assimilate all the new and useful views into one overall manual of selling excellence: they all teach each other.

But look at what that simple exercise is also teaching: they have to have ego strength to share their insights with the group; they open their views and insights to criticism and feedback; they have to monitor, measure, experiment, and then critically evaluate. They also have to look at both the useful and not so useful points. And, finally, they then teach their colleagues, work as a unit searching for solutions and new and better ways of doing things: it's all management, experimentation, cooperation, innovation, and more.

Incentivize your managers to teach, coach, mentor, and develop the people around them; reorient or remove those who don't. The leadership role – to coin a well-worn phrase – is supposed to create more people who will exhibit leadership tomorrow, not more followers. Lead by example yourself. Show them how to get the main points across and, more importantly, how to listen and thereby learn themselves. Gather all the knowledge – fine-tune it. If people in the organization are not sharing insights, contacts, lessons, tricks, then the knowledge and skill levels become skewed toward individuals rather than the organization as a whole. People with knowledge become powerful and – over time – they can become problematic. Sharing the knowledge avoids this.

Get Them Solving Their Own Problems

A huge part of developing a person is to give them confidence, encouragement, support, and to push them toward becoming independent. Doing so makes *your* life so much easier. There's nothing worse than a clingy employee: they take up so much of your time and zap both your energy and focus.

There's a fine line to be walked between getting people to solve their own problems and them holding back refusing to sound the alarm simply because they can't think up a solution all by themselves. Be very aware of this. A lot of gurus and management types pontificate about refusing to listen to a problem unless the person bringing it also brings suggested solutions. The potentially lethal downside to this is that you lose valuable time while others dither or obey your rule: "I'm not telling him. He'll go nuts because I can't think of any solution to it".

Asking questions without suggesting the answers is your first step: the Socratic Approach again. Get people to talk out their thinking. Don't spoon-feed the answers to them: let them work it out for themselves. Your questions should guide them.

Next, ask questions about the answers they give. Get them thinking things through fully. Do this in a non-judgmental way. Work the boards to keep track of the points they make. Keep your tone of voice calm and relaxed. Don't act superior like you know they're wrong or anything like that. Remember: encourage, support, assist.

The more you do this the more people can move beyond their frustrations or anger – or any emotion blinding them – and contribute to group meetings and discussions in more meaningful ways. In time, they move from you asking questions to asking questions themselves in order to reach the solutions by themselves.

Don't allow personal attacks or hurtful criticisms. Keep it all constructive and meaningful. Again, it should only take a little extra time and not overly distract you from your day, but the benefits – increased attention, involvement, engagement, competency, confidence, self-esteem, commitment - far outweigh the extra effort on your part.

Leverage Their Reciprocity

The human tendency toward reciprocity is very powerful. Trained negotiators know this only too well and leverage it to their advantage. Very often, a trained negotiator will give a little knowing the other side will reciprocate. But here's the trick: the negotiator gives away or concedes what costs him nothing but what the other side views as highly valuable - it's about as simple as that. We see businesses doing this too with free gifts or restaurants with free bread rolls or whatever; the gifts or free food cost little if anything to produce yet the customers value them so much higher than the cost to produce them. The customers then reciprocate by giving, in money, far more than the 'free' item cost the business or restaurant.

Show someone a small kindness or do them a small favor (small to you but big and meaningful to them) and eventually they'll reciprocate. They may take your side, or work extra hours, or back a plan, or talk others around to siding with you. The point is this: research shows that people often reciprocate in a *disproportionate* way. In other words, they often return favors bigger than the ones granted to them. Bear this in mind!

Some Final Thoughts

Everything – at some point – must go through people. There's no sense in having employees arriving to work everyday and not leveraging their abilities, connections – and more: you're just leaving money on the table when you indulge in silly behavior like that.

Employees are often so much more capable than just the pigeon-holed job titles we push them into. Again, interacting and engaging with people by walking around enables you to discover whether or not people are in the right jobs or capable of offering so much more than you are currently getting from them. My advice to you: go find out! Leverage what you can and manage how you put it to best use. Create new and valuable cross-functional, rank-transcending, job-title-busting, and multi-disciplinary synergies. Empower yourself by connecting with those who work with you. Then leverage what you can to put yourself ahead of the pack and the business on the best course. Why opt for the alternative of the same old same old? Plug into other peoples networks, contacts, knowledge.

There are several things you must never overlook about people:

1. They are *always* motivated;
2. They are *always* creative;
3. They are *always* talking;
4. They are *always* watching;
5. They are *always* listening;
6. They are *always* thinking and feeling...

Your job is to get them motivated into doing what *you* need them to do, leverage their creativity to the benefit of the organization, and ensure their complaints are spoken to *you* and not customers/clients or external web blogs.[77]

Always make sure you know *how* to delegate, *when* to delegate, *what* to delegate, and *to whom*. Then, start delegating!

Be certain your organizational knowledge map is not based entirely on job description. Many people have skills they're never asked to use at work.

Look for ways to incentivize your managers to teach, guide, mentor, develop. Make it a part of their daily job. If they're not developing the next generation of managers, what are they doing there?

---

[77] The amount of bitching some employees of all ranks do on Facebook, for example, can be staggering!

Never forget that everything you do or don't do serves as an example for others. These examples build up over time to define organizational norms: accepted behavior - culture. To change behavior, you have to change norms – and you change norms by changing the examples you and your management team set daily; incentivizing the changes and installing metrics and methodologies to keep everything in line.

Chapter 9
Manage & Lead Them

Your thinking forms your perspective which guides your attitude and ultimately determines your behavior; people then react to your behavior or attitude – we saw this when look at the Pygmalion and Golem effects earlier. Leading and managing people become easier when you get your approach play and mental perspective right: always start with You; do not damage your personal leadership brand in the eyes of those around you.

Start with yourself first; then get your senior team right; then allow positive example setting, engaging people by walking around, and interacting with employees become the norm. Doing so ensures all the right people are on the bus, sitting in the right seats, doing what they do best, listening and interacting with everyone to create positive synergies, building trust and motivation and generating commitment and buy-in. You don't need to indulge time wasting or long irrelevant conversations when seeking to engage with others, but you must do it; remember: in the long-run laziness never pays, it *always* costs!

Questions to Become Effective

Here are some simple guidelines to keep in mind when seeking to manage people in an effective way:

> Question 1: How will what you are about to say motivate and/or help the person you are dealing with get their job done or develop into a more capable employee?

Stop and think: excellent preparation is an inbuilt habit you should seek to cultivate. Too often we allow the situation dictate our reactions and govern our emotions; don't allow it to. Even if you are pulling an employee up for not performing, consider upfront how what you are going to say can get the message across but in such a way as to kick start an improvement in them rather than lead to them silently fuming. Don't spend all day at it, but do show them the result, what was expected, the gap, how it impacts on everyone around them, and then get *them* to suggest how they might close the gap: seek participation, commitment, and buy-in from them. Seek to help, not punish.

> Question 2: Are you about to get in your own way and foul things up?

Check your perspective, your attitude, your tone, your body language; always start with You. Do you have all the facts? Where did you get them from or whom did you hear them from? Remember, most of what stands in any manager's way emanates from that manager him/herself. Often, when we are tired, we drop our guard, get lazy with our body language and tone of voice, and end up communicating something we didn't intend to. Stay alert to getting in your own way and alienating others thereby ultimately damaging your own leadership brand in the eyes of those around you.

Question 3: Is what you are talking about important to the employee? If not, how can you make it so?

Incentives are *not* about money and meeting targets no matter what all the other experts out there tell you. Incentives are about 'behavior'. The desired end profits come about as secondary results to the underlying behavior. If an employee cannot appreciate or associate with what you are saying, you're wasting your time. You must make what you say appeal to the person you are talking to. Use language and analogies from *their* world, not yours, when you seek to motivate them.

Question 4: Will the incentives you offer or the speech you give actually create the desired behavior you are seeking or might other behavior pop-up instead?

This is important. The world is littered with examples of people behaving in bizarre ways just to beat the system, meet the metrics, get the bonus. If you pay based on timely or fast delivery, don't be surprised if that creates behaviors that pick up speeding tickets. If you incentivize people for the number of mortgages on the books or loans given out, don't be surprised if that prompts the type of behavior whereby loans are given out to people who ultimately cannot afford to pay them if interest rates shift just a little. If you dock marks from students' grades for not turning up to boring lectures, don't be surprised if they arrive but spend the class asleep or surfing the internet. Very often, we unwittingly install systems and processes that reward *bad* behavior!

Question 5: Are you clear when telling them what you want and expect?

Remember: everything stands or falls on communication; poor and ineffective communication is at the root of most human problems - world, political, social, and family. Speak their language, use analogies they can associate with, hit the key points and make sure they heard and understood those key points.

Question 6: Are you willing to seek *their* input in the matter?

Context is the ultimate deciding factor in whether you involve them or not and to what extent. Does the business have the time to get everyone involved? This is not about how busy *you* are: it's about whether the business is in trouble or the context is demanding swift action. As a general rule of thumb, anything that directly impacts upon employees – how they operate – should see you seeking their input. Doing so lowers resistance, shows you are willing to listen to their concerns, and more.

Question 7: Can you allow them to work toward the solution themselves?

Guide them. Ask questions that stimulate their thinking and enable them to critically evaluate a situation. Develop them. Be sensible and manage time: this is not about handing over the keys of the asylum to the lunatics or spending all day on something simple. It may simply be a team of managers you are guiding and developing who in turn will do the same with the layer of personnel beneath them. At no point am I advocating you must talk with each and every person in a 20,000 person organization every day!

Question 8: Are you focusing on the task?

Emphasize the gap in actual versus desired results, how it impacts on everyone, and then seek suggestions on how they might close the gap. Keep their ego and defensiveness out of it by talking about the task and not the person.

Question 9: Have you put your positive intent upfront?

Many employees are suspicious when a manager suddenly shows an interest in something or raises a problem that requires attention. You need to work hard and constantly to dampen down their suspicions and negative expectations. Don't get in your own way: prepare, check your tone and mood, focus on the task, aim to motivate and work toward a solution, be clear, and make sure you bring about the desired behavior and not some bizarre alternative.

Question 10: Have you communicated clearly that you are future- and solution-oriented and that you expect the very same in return?

The first part helps to relieve the pressure and expectation that you are out to get them: you are avoiding blame for the past and looking to find a positive way forward. The second part shows that it is a two-way street: you are demanding cooperative interaction from them. They get to have an intelligent say, to shape the ultimate solution: employees have a role to play in being managed.

Question 11: Have you prepared?

When you get caught not knowing the basics, now knowing your stuff, your credibility suffers. This does not mean you play the know-it-all. But you do need to prepare: Who will be there? What might you expect? How will you play things out? In what order should you mention things? Remember, laziness *never* pays: it *always* costs.

Question 12: Are you Context aware?

Getting managers to a point where they are "Context Intelligent" was a major theme in book 1 of this series.[78] Sauntering into an office or building with a particular message to deliver ignorant of the context into which you are walking can see you looking foolish, insensitive, or downright conniving. What if, for example, someone just got passed over for promotion or suffered a personal tragedy and you've arrived to give them a talk about upping their performance? They won't be very interested! The talk may be very necessary but it needs to come at another time.

Question 13: Are you constantly reassessing?

Always hold in the back of your mind the awareness that you don't know everything, can't hear about everything, and

---

[78] McCormack (2008) chapter 7.

may simply get blindsided once in a while – nobody can prepare for *every*thing in business and management. Monitor the mood, the body language, the facial expressions. Do people seem to be with you or are they bored, skeptical, angry? Switch on and tune in. Always be ready to switch gears, to take the ball and run with it, or to keep your powder dry. Constantly reassess the context in which you are standing or walking into.

How to End Micro-Management

In many ways, micro-management is simply a matter of perspective and structure. You can defeat it via 'Flagging' and 'Check-Back'.

'Flagging' simply means, for example, "If daily sales drop below $12,000 for four straight days or more, let me know". This enables you to stay on top of things without standing over an employee reading their charts with them.

'Check-Back' is a method you can use to monitor something without the appearance of micro-managing the person. Let's say your performance lately has been sub par. After chatting with you about it and agreeing upon ways to improve it, I might say something like, "Okay, let's try that and we'll meet each Friday morning at 10am for the next few weeks to see how this new approach is working out". Now you know I'll be dipping in and out. If I didn't tell you this, then my simple act of looking over your shoulder every Friday morning might make you feel uncomfortable.

Flagging and Check-Back change a person's perspective. They know when to raise the alarm. Your involvement in the matter will not come as a surprise or shock to them. Telling people you will look in once a week – if done correctly - moves you from unexpected intruder to expected guest. It moves you from "watching" to "interested and willing to help".

The Darker Side of Management

Far too many books tell you how to use frameworks and models to better the organization and the people around you. But the truth is this: once you know how to use a thing you don't always have to use it for overtly saintly purposes.

Let's go back to the Five Constituencies. It's not all about managing yourself so that you don't have an adverse impact on all the constituencies around you: it's also about influencing or manipulating those constituencies to your benefit. If I know that a bit of showmanship on my part will get around to everyone really quickly, then I might use that to my advantage: using the organizational grapevine to play organizational politics. So, you can fake anger – or any other emotion - occasionally to bring about a desired effect.

This is why I refer to leadership as the management of higher order things as opposed to a totally separate form of human being – the 'Leader'. The deliberately timed display to the Five Constituencies is simply a leadership activity from a person to effect how others perceive him, how they view him on a particular matter, what they think of him at that moment, knowing they will spread a particular message for him – he is *managing* himself and *managing* others in an intelligent and deliberate way: all great leadership.

Use Dramatization

A picture says a thousand words, and so too does an image or a dramatization. There's a huge difference between me saying "...and if that happens the business will collapse", and me saying exactly the same thing but pushing a tall object on the desk over as the words "will collapse" come out. The message via the dramatization and imagery has a far bigger impact on the person watching than simple words alone.

Knowing this gives you two key benefits. First, you can use this to your advantage when seeking to convince and influence people. Second, you can recognize when this technique is being used *against* you by someone else.

A little dramatization – some light showmanship – properly done with good timing can leave a far better lasting impact than words alone. This is why preparation is so crucial. You need to plan the dramatization to ensure maximum effect, perfect timing, and to ensure it all looks natural.

Manage What You Measure

Granted, not all things of value are capable of precise measurement. Nonetheless, a huge answer to organizational problems can be found in: (1) a failure to set expectations, goals, targets; (2) a failure to clearly communicate those expectations, and (3) a failure to enforce those expectations – Set-Communicate-Enforce.

People in the organization must know what is expected of them. It is for you to ensure your communication is crystal clear. And you must hold them to these expectations. Don't be afraid of conflict. Don't be afraid of being unpopular or disliked. Don't focus on how you're spoiling your relationship with the other person. People always have a "good reason" for not meeting a target. You must be able to point out underperformance without allowing any personal friendship to cloud the issue and you must be able to do this without attacking the self-esteem or dignity of the person. Remember, a person is *not* their performance – make sure they, too, realize this.

Where possible and sensible, to get people to buy into your expectations, give them input into the goal or target setting. At the very least let them see *why* you are setting such expectations and how you came up with them. Transparency, open

179

discussion, and input, help to generate buy-in and commitment and lessen any resistance to what you are setting out.

Manage Your Meetings

"Death by meeting" – how often have you heard *that* one?! Meetings often provide two functions: (1) they bore people to death and waste time; (2) they enable people to escape, feel important, and drone on and on for hours.

If a meeting doesn't have a real purpose, it shouldn't be happening. Too often meetings become habit, fixed in the schedule, expected. If there's no point, don't go, don't hold one, scrap it from the daily routine.

Let people know about the meeting upfront. Get them to prepare ahead of time and share with them any information required to enable better preparation and a more effective meeting. Don't suggest any solutions. You don't want to prejudice their thinking. You want constructive participation, brainstorming, idea generation, solution building.

Keep the people positive. When they get stuck on a problem or pessimistic point of view, unstick them by asking a question. Guide them. You yourself may not know the answer or the solution but that does not mean you cannot manage them – and yourself – toward a better outcome.

Most of us leave a meeting with "so what?" rattling around in the back of our minds. There are three key ingredients to end a meeting: (1) summarize what was discussed and agreed; (2) state what will be done before meeting again; and (3) state accountability and responsibility – *who* must do those things and by *when*. Ending this way adds reason to the whole meeting having occurred in the first place and gives a meaningful and worthwhile reason for the next meeting.

Focus on the Solution, *not* on the Problem

Recognize a problem. Accept and admit that it exists. But don't dwell or focus on it too long: doing so simply drains your energy and impacts negatively upon attitude and morale.

Move quickly toward discussing possible solutions. Use "How?" a lot and keep using "How?" for your first five sentences to change the mood - a solution-oriented mindset kick-starts creativity and keeps people positive. Problem-oriented mindsets close our eyes to opportunities and ways out of our problems.

Personally, I tend to walk away and let an issue sit in the back of my mind for a day or two. It's when I'm off doing something else that I often come up with the solution. Taking time away from a tough problem, or a big risk, or a failure, can allow your subconscious to mull over the issue for a while and give you time to reframe and change perspective.

Censorship Cubed

Once they've arrived prepared and start discussing the issues, make sure you separate the generation of ideas and the feasibility of suggestions into two distinct and separate time frames. This is key in brainstorming: focus on what you want first and then deal with what's possible later.

If people are editing each other's suggestions as they're made, they may inadvertently bring about what I term Censoring Cubed. Let us say you make a creative suggestion but I instantly shoot it down. I've censored you, i.e. I've shut you up and edited what you said. From that point forward, you might decide that making additional contributions to the meeting is simply not worth the hassle: you are now censoring or silencing yourself. Others watching your idea being shot down might also decide to stay quiet – a third layer of censoring (me, you, them);

and all from one idiotic person leading the discussion: Censorship Cubed! Not just censored three times, but cubed – each has a multiplier effect

This kind of ineffective behavior on the part of me leading the discussion often leads to the scrapping of a good idea before it is fully explored and/or cause people to go quiet for fear of suggesting workable solutions that may simply be dismissed as silly ideas.

And you can guess the result, right? I – the ineffective "leader" – ram home my own opinions; maintain the status quo; prevent meaningful change; go tell the other "leaders" that I asked for suggestions but got little to none! How many times have we seen that occur!!

Navigating the Either-Or Traps

I hate this: "You're either with us or against us". You'll come across this kind of statement in so many walks of life. It has been used by sales people, managers, CEOs, and American Presidents.

The reason I hate such statements is because they are psychological traps. They immediately force you to wrongly conclude you only have *two* choices available to you. Not only that, they use the weight of social proof – and the threat of exclusion from your group of pals or colleagues – to force you to take the side they want you to take.

You rarely have only two choices. But having been brought up on adrenalin-style *fight or flight* thinking, perhaps it is understandable why the Either-Or Trap is so effective.[79]

And here's the remedy: stay calm, recognize what's going on, and ask for or think up a third option. I never accept an

---

[79] See Grossman (1995) who advocates expanding the two choices in combat scenarios to four: Fight, Flight, Posture, and Submit.

either-or ultimatum. I like to think I'm a little more creative than the person confronting me with such a trick. And you should be too.

Never assume people making such statements are less intelligent or creative than you: they may simply be using the darker side of a management technique against you. They may actually know precisely what they're doing: they're trying to *manage* you! Remember, good management is about recognizing what's going on: you need to be Context Intelligent and People-Wise. Recognize when someone is using a trick like this against you and be aware that you in turn can use it against others to meet your own ends.

Learn to 'Bookmark' Conversations

Working the boards – as we saw earlier – is an excellent way of keeping people in a room on topic, delivering focused value in meetings, and preventing them from running down tangents and off point. But as a manager, you also need to be able to do all of this *without* the boards.

Trial lawyers are good at this. "Yes, that's all well and good, but you still haven't answered my question about…" That, right there, is the skill you're looking to fine tune. Stay focused on the point. You went into the conversation – hopefully – with an end objective in mind. Anything that does not take you toward that objective needs to be sidelined. Here's an example of an actual conversation I had with a person many years ago:

Me: You told me you had the authority to do this. Now it turns out that was not the case. So, everything after that point must fall into question.

Manager: I don't like being called a liar.

Me: I'm not calling you a liar.

Manager: Yes you are. You just said I lied about having authority. I thought I did. Others with my title have done this kind of thing before. I don't see why they should be treated one way and me another.

Okay, let's stop right there for a moment. This is how people can ramble, allow emotion to take over, and bring a whole list of other unaired grievances into a conversation. The danger here is that I follow him down the "liar", "others" "treated one way and me another" tangents.

Follow now as I keep this guy on track:

Me: My point to you is this: if you didn't actually have the authority, then we have to look carefully at everything else that follows after that point. Do you agree?

Manager: No I don't. I don't like being called a liar.

Me: It's simply due process and good law. It's what other good companies do. We have to make sure that everything in your report was obtained properly and will not cause us problems further down the line. I never called you a liar: that's something you've read into what I'm saying but I'm telling you to your face that you're mishearing and misreading me on that. We need to cover ourselves with this report or you could find yourself in a lot of hot water later.

Manager: So what exactly do you want to look at?

See how the manager tried to keep me on the "liar" track? But I did a number of things.

First, I depersonalized the issue by pointing to proper due process and the law. Second, I introduced comparison by pointing to what other top companies do. Third, I focus on the report – not on him – and introduce the idea of him avoiding personal pain later. Fourth, I briefly return to the "liar" issue to deal with it once and for all. Fifth, I then move quickly back onto what I want to deal with – the main issue – by repeating the "pain" issue and using "we" while focusing on the report and *not* on him. Sixth, I never use "but" because this – as we saw earlier – can act as a barrier to progress. Seven, referring to other companies and such takes *me* out of the role of bad guy so that communication between the two of us becomes less strained; if anything, I'm the friendly warning trying to protect him from a common foe.

Humans are very skilled at using emotion to draw you in: they've been doing it all their lives – it is hardwired into their brains. Manipulation can come so naturally to so many people. Your job as a manager is to stay calm, recognize the tricks being used on you, to step back and disconnect emotionally to see what is really going on, and to stick to the point. If the other issues won't go away, commit to returning to them in another conversation later - bookmark your conversations and/or work the boards. Allowing yourself to run with the other person down the tangents equates to you disempowering yourself: don't willingly walk unprepared into an ambush. You've prepared for *this* conversation: manage it and see it through.

If You Must Rush, Rush *Intelligently*

In the business world, there's a difference between "speed" and "haste".[80]

---

[80] For a more detailed discussion on speed in business, see: Jennings et al (2000, 2002).

Speed is the intelligent version of rushing. Speed suggests care, deliberate movement, end goals in sight, thinking. Haste, on the other hand, suggests going off half-cocked, not thinking, bursting out the gate without knowing where you're headed to.

As we saw earlier, for different messages you need different channels: sending an urgent message through the same channel as other messages will simply see it getting lost among all the other stuff. So when in a rush, do so in an intelligent way: always choose "speed" over "haste".

Manage the Blame Shifters

You'll always encounter what I term "Blame Shifters". Depending on how often they shift blame, these people can range from once-off-ers to total wasters.

"Yeah, I didn't get around to it because something came up", is the usual line from such people. In essence, the guy didn't do what he was supposed to do. "Something" immediately alerts you to be on your guard: either this was so personal he can't mention it or he's trying to shift the blame onto something completely vague and irrelevant. A lot of passive-aggressive people behave this way; rather than state disagreement upfront (aggressive) they turn up late or lose things or conveniently forget or get distracted (passive).

Having employees with this behavior hardwired into their brains simply means they'll never put the organization or department or team first. They're like spoiled kids expecting mommy or daddy to cave in as soon as they hear they encountered the smallest of difficulties or distractions. If as a manager you cannot hold employees to their commitments, to deadlines, to targets and goals, to their responsibilities – you've got problems. Remember, blame is simply a way of shifting and/or denying responsibility. That's *not* a trait you want in the people you are relying on to get the job done. If it's evident in your senior team, stomp it out *fast*!

Manage these people by disarming them *before* they even try to do battle with you: "...and if anything comes up or you encounter difficulties, get back to me fast". It's the "get back to me fast" part that kills off their blame shifting. Now you've mentioned the possibility of a distraction *before* they have *and* you've told them what to do if this occurs. You've applied an extra layer of glue to accountability for the task: they're stuck with it for sure - there's no weaseling out of it. You don't care how good a story someone comes up with for not doing what they were supposed to do. Get them to tell you the story first and then move on to achieve the desired results, not the other – and more usual – way around: no result but hey, I've got a great story to explain why not!

As always, start with *You*. Is your system and general way of doing things making people look like Blame Shifters when really they're not? You're the one exercising leadership – go find out!

Manage Their Anger

Some people are angry: it's a fact of life. They may have worked there for years and kept it all bottled up inside. You shouldn't be surprised if seeking their views is a new occurrence for them and if some of them use that as an opportunity to vent about things you probably never even heard of.

Sometimes you just have to sit back and let them get it off their chest at first – the old rule of never interrupt an angry man. They'll ramble, run down tangents and blind alleys, and you may even find yourself thinking "What have I done?" as the person does a pantomime act right in front of you. After a while, get the person to slow down. Slow their words. Tell them you're listening but they're going too fast and starting to ramble. Slowing them down gets them to think and it has a calming effect thereby neutralizing the emotion. Make sure *you* also stay calm – in life, the first to lose his temper often ends up as the loser. Don't get drawn in by any personal attack or criticism, any excuse-making or shocking revelations. As humans, we generally respond in kind: anger in one person can spark an angry response from another.

There are two smart rules when it comes to anger: (1) don't criticize a person when *you* are angry, and (2) don't criticize a person when *they* are angry. Doing so means you are dealing from a closed mind position or playing into one. If it's that important now it will be just as important tomorrow: there's a big difference between "delaying" versus "retreating".

Also try to use words to diffuse anger before or after it surfaces. Saying something along the lines of, "I know you're experienced enough not to get angry when I tell you that…", is one way of killing anger before it even gets a chance to surface. Note how this sentence compliments the person, makes them feel important and accomplished. More importantly, after delivering the compliment I avoid wiping it from their memory by not using "but" immediately afterwards.

Try, "I seem to have made a mess of this by saying something or putting it in a way that is making you angry", if anger has already surfaced. Note what this sentence is trying to do: I immediately take the blame while at the same time deliberately – but subtly – drawing their awareness to their own anger.

There are of course limits. People are allowed to express anger but not to disrespect you – others should see from your demeanor that, while you will allow them vent a little, you are not about to become a doormat or spectacle for onlookers. If you think you're in danger, get out of there! In time, you need to develop people to the point where they can vent without endangering those around them or creating a sense of alarm. Manage it: tell someone you're giving them a chance to vent but they must do it in a calm way so as to enable you to help them and to help them help themselves.

Manage Their Appearance

We've already touched on this earlier. Always remember this – how you dress has a two-way effect: on the people looking at you and on *you* yourself. And it's important for your employees too. People looking at them will form an impression of your business within the first few seconds, often before a word is even spoken. A failure on your part – and on the part of each of your employees – to *manage* that impression will simply see blame migrate to *you*.

When managing the appearance of the people around you – and when managing your own appearance - always remember class. I've watched young kids going to court to answer criminal charges. People looking at them would think, "Wow, what a scumbag. He couldn't even dress properly for the judge". And yet, when you looked closely, that poor kid was probably wearing his "best" jeans and his "best" tee-shirt. But, in terms of class, jeans are just jeans no matter how expensive. That kid would have done better in a cheap secondhand suit than in jeans worth ten times more.

Managing appearance manages perception and assumptions which in turn manage willingness to do business with your organization. There's no point having a brilliant solution wrapped up in a wonderful presentation if the person delivering it looks like a lazy disrespectful waster.

Managing Your Boss

I am always saddened by the number of people I encounter every year who make no effort to lead in an upward direction.[81] For many, the thought of managing their boss sounds totally alien. But, just like example setting, managing and leading should spread out in all directions and not just cascade down to those below.

Sometimes you have to criticize your boss. Sometimes he gets things wrong, is pig-headed, or just doesn't get it. Framing your conversation as information you just discovered that could save him from embarrassment or from making a mistake is one way to go. It doesn't come across as a criticism of him per se. Move him from accepting or rejecting *criticism* to a position of accepting or rejecting *information*: no ego or defensiveness required on his part.

Another route is to go back to the power of "Ask". Instead of coming straight out and telling him that he's the jerk causing all the problems, frame your conversation in the form of a question: play dumb. Tell him you don't know why something is going wrong and use questions to both guide him and to avoid appearing to point the finger of criticism at him. A third way is to create conventional wisdom – we saw this earlier – and get someone else to point it out to him.

Whether framing your conversation as information or a question, or using others as a conduit, the aim is to ensure you disengage his ego, prevent him from becoming defensive, and ensure you get what you need without damaging the working relationship. This can only be done by knowing a person's thinking style, their aims, and communicating with them in their own language to play to how they process information - some love to hear information; others shoot the messenger: knowing the people around you includes those above you too!

---

[81] You can bully in an upward direction too!

Managing Customers and Clients

"The customer is always right" must surely be one of the most dangerous adages in the world of business. And here are some of the reasons I don't buy into that kind of thinking:

- You surrender power;
- You decrease respect for you and your position;
- You invite people to treat you like a doormat;
- You encourage the worst of peoples' behavior;
- There is no 50-50 solution generation or coming together of minds on a level playing field of mutual respect;
- In extreme cases, you perpetuate a cycle of stupidity thereby
  - Alienating your own workers;
  - Warping the organizational culture;
  - Creating unprofitable customers;
  - Ignoring profitable customers.

The adage, while noble in sentiment, has potentially severe and harmful limits. Simply put: it's not true! More often than not, the customer is wrong![82] If you ever spent one hour working on the ground in retail you would know this beyond a shadow of a doubt. So be aware that there are times when you must manage your customers or clients. A small minority of them, if they get their way or you give in to them, cause more harm than good. They take up too much time, alienate your workers, cost too much to service, and distract you from dealing with the good and valuable customers. That's *not* the way to run a business. Remember, managing spreads out in all directions to all Five Constituencies. Occasionally you must safeguard the loyalty of your own employees to you by dropping your own loyalty to an abusive or overly demanding customer or client.

---

[82] Granted, while the customer may not always be right, he *is* the customer.

A Method for Doing the Impossible

Setting up your own business, running your own department, steering an entire organization – any number of scenarios – will see you confronted with situations that can be incredibly daunting and for which you very often don't have the slightest clue as to the solution or how to go about tackling the issue. But there is a very simple approach you can use – one that uses "Ask" – and here it is: Ask "how" – then walk away! It's as simple as that. Let me draw it out for you below:

Remember, asking "How?" does not mean that you yourself must have the answer first. This is about pushing yourself as well as those around you. As we said earlier, asking questions can be a very effective method of developing people: it's also very effective for developing yourself and reaching for discovery and solutions. So, first step: Ask "How?" because:

- It opens the door to creativity. It enables you to start from a position of possibility and openness. Don't put the full stop at the start of your sentence! "How" is an *open* question!
- Not starting with "How?" but instead giving in or stating something can't be done simply gives you an excuse not to try and this excuse – whether relied upon immediately or later – is tantamount to giving yourself psychological permission to fail. The really tragic aspect to all of this is that people generally don't even realize when they are dis-empowering themselves along these lines.

Once you have asked "How?" can something be done, or overcome, or dealt with…you walk away. And you walk away without having come up with any answers. It's a question you put to those around you and to yourself: How? And here's why you then walk away after posing such a question:

- Walking away allows you to sulk for a while if you are so inclined, to throw a tantrum, to sink into the depths of depression and disappointment if you must; always give yourself a time-out to regroup, recharge, and re-psyche yourself no matter who or what is screaming for an immediate solution;
- Walking away and turning your mind to other things – or simply going for a walk or returning to the issue a few days later – allows your subconscious to work on it. Often when you walk away from something for a few days, you encounter parts of the solution in people's conversations, in things on TV, or in mere bolts out of the blue. As Renoir put it: you have to know how to loaf a bit;[83]
- And as all these things are working for you, the same is happening for all the other people that were in the room when you threw the 'How?' question out onto the table. You should all return with creativity buzzing.

The Five- M's of Intelligent Managerial Behavior

Measure. You cannot manage what you do not measure. Oh sure, some things are incapable of accurate measurement according to many people (happiness, resistance, resentment…) but you *can* measure everything around or related to such issues: time, regularity, number of people i.e. I don't know the size of the rock you just threw into the pond, but I *can* measure the size of the ripples every time! If you don't do something as simple as mark the start date for your new diet in your calendar, after two weeks you'll think you've been on it a month – it's as simple as that! The same with how long a person has been complaining, or how long the bank manager is taking to get

---

[83] Taken from Kingston (2003) as quoted earlier.

back to you, or how long…if you're not measuring such things you're not managing the impact they have on your thinking, your perspective, your mood, and your consequent behavior.

Monitor. Lots of companies measure lots of things. Many, however, don't monitor the figures closely. We see this in our personal lives: the blind eye turned to the credit card debt, the bank account, the amount we pay out on car and life insurance. We get statements measuring all these things numerous times a year and yet careful monitoring would see many of us in far better positions than we are right now. And it's the same in business. How often do you look at the figures, the measures, the metrics, the ratios? How often *should* you look at them? Do you get your P&L account once per year from your accountant or weekly to stay right on top of developments? All the fancy measures in the world are totally and utterly useless if you're not looking at them regularly – and "regularly" is a word you need to define very carefully for yourself especially if you're just not a numbers person (which most of us are not!).

Mention. As soon as you spot something   good, bad, or inexplicable – bring it up: out it to bring attention to it and to get people looking and thinking. If a person's performance is dropping, or their absenteeism climbing, or their sales numbers tanking, or sales per hour or shrinkage or delivery times or customer satisfaction or hits to the website or bank fees or investment fees or job applications…are changing in either direction or simply staying the same, be aware of it, form an intelligent view on it, and manage it.

Motivate. You don't always have to give fancy speeches to get people on board. The act of measuring, monitoring, and mentioning will very often in themselves provide the motivation for people to move or correct course. If their incentives are linked to such things in an intelligent way, all the better. If the general employees do not measure and monitor such things, then you mentioning it is the first step toward motivating people to get back on track or to correct course.

Move. Often you have to take corrective measures to get things back on track, to avoid looming disaster or to take advantage of a developing opportunity. If you don't monitor what you're measuring you won't see these things coming. And if you don't mention them you won't have intelligent debate, analysis or insights into what to do about them nor will you have provided sufficient motivation for people to get off their asses and start putting things right.

These Five Ms are a continuous cycle. After Move, you return to Monitor again. Once in a while, Constantly Reassess the actual Measures in place – are they still pertinent, relevant, necessary? Remain Context Sensitive on this front. Remember: manage the data - don't let *it* manage *you*!

Some Final Thoughts

Managing people is so much easier when you get your approach-play right: Preparation and You. Always start with yourself. Nothing you do, don't do, say, don't say…should lead to you making your own life and the management of people around you more difficult. We covered incisive questions in this chapter that aid here.

When you talk, do you motivate people and talk about things they understand and care about? Do your managers do the same?

Resolve from now on to make Preparation a cornerstone for everything you do: conversations, presentations – interactions of any form. Have an aim, speak their language, get it done.

Stop wasting time in meetings. From now on ask if there's a real need for the meeting. Then get it done and over with fast. Stay focused throughout, give a brief recap of what was discussed, and end with a list of things to be achieved by the next meeting (if another is required) and determine who is to do these things.

Start avoiding the Either/Or Trap by demanding or searching for a minimum of three choices to the important obstacles or issues you encounter; you must be flexible - rigidity kills!

When stuck, ask "How?" and then walk away for a while: Block negativity and allow creativity a chance to develop.

Never forget that you are also out to manage the *perceptions* of those around you. Micro management doesn't have to look like micro management! The use of dramatization in intelligent ways enhances aspects of your arguments. The 5-Ms – Measure, Monitor, Mention, Motivate, and Move – can all impact how an issue is viewed or dealt with: motivation and behavior turn positive.

Your ability to "Work the Boards" is something that should develop into "Book Marking Conversations" and ultimately to managing your meetings and the people around you. It *all* starts with an ability to manage yourself and a willingness to prepare upfront and Constantly Reassess as you move forward. (Go back to book one – *The 'YOU' Factor: If You Cannot Manage Yourself, You Cannot Manage Others* – if necessary). Managing people – just like setting suitable examples - is something that spreads out to all Five Constituencies, starting and ending with You. Managing your boss, your customers/clients, your stakeholders – all the key constituencies around you – often becomes a daily necessity.

Chapter 10
From Power to Influence

Forms of Power

Power is not simply a matter of position, status, or rank. A failure on your part to recognize this can see you walking yourself into unnecessary problems.

That old grump who's been with the company for years but never held a managerial position probably has more power than a lot of the managers around him: it's the power of longevity of service; the power of persisting presence; the power of knowledge and organizational politics. He probably knows how the place runs better than everyone else. He knows who to connect with, who gets things done, and who to watch out for. Should you ignore him? Attack him? Remove him? Seek his assistance?

One of the dangers of power is that a person getting it often starts talking more and listening less. Remember; you can only ever speak what you already know; you stop learning! This takes us back to the old adage: you have one mouth and two ears; use them in that proportion! Therefore, we can say that getting power can change behavior in an unhelpful way: less listening, more talking. And since everything we are concerned about in leadership and management revolves around – or is underpinned by – behavior, this makes power a vital concern to any would-be *effective* manager.

Depending on who you ask, there is anything from half a dozen to an infinite number of different forms of power.

The obvious one is *Position* power. We all know who the CEO is and who the managers are. And yet, their behavior and characteristics can often serve to dis-empower themselves; we all know the manager who hates confrontation, or hates to disappoint people, or hates to lose friends, or deliver unpopular news. We often refer to these people as limp-wristed managers, spineless or gutless cowards.

The next form of power easily recognized as humans is *Coercive* power or the power to punish: We remember this from childhood. Who in your organization can punish others? Who can punish *you*? Who can you punish? We can also take a sneaky approach here and consider the question of who can you make *believe* is subject to punishment from you? In other words, can you create an aura that appears to give you more power than you actually have? Is anyone doing this to you?

The ability to *Reward* is another form of power. Very often the person dishing out the appraisals, bonuses, doing the hiring, making the promotion decisions, is a person others bow to simply because such people have the power to make or break a career. This is important to watch for as you walk around on a daily basis throughout the year: who are people sucking up to, is this sucking up getting in the way of other things, and is the person with the power abusing it or wearing it well?

We all know that knowledge is power; we've heard that adage all our lives. And this is important: knowledge enables a person to have power over people *above* him or her in the organizational chain. You've probably witnessed this already in your own job: a person the managers can't budge because he or she is the only person who knows how to do a thing or has been doing it for so long he's viewed as an expert on it. This is why open dialogue, engaging with people, and then sharing the knowledge throughout the entire organization are of fundamental importance. Not only does such an approach benefit the business as a whole – it aids in preventing the rise of powerful individuals: the rising tide of knowledge must lift *all* boats.

Behavior and attitude can also create forms of power. We all know the grump, or the person who'll snap your head off. We also know the people who don't take any nonsense. What's amazing about these people is that you'll often find no-one wants to screw with them – not even the people above them in the organization. Think about it: I being an absolute crank and anti-Christ – my behavior – can cause you to deliberately alter *your* behavior even if you're my boss!

Organizational charts rarely tell you who holds the *real* power. Such charts don't tell you how things get done, who helps or hinders. Knowledge maps are often constructed on position and title rather than true ability. Figures tell you the end result but not the reason why, or the lost or negative synergies, or how to make things better. Be aware of the differing forms of power - who holds them, how they exercise them (Propensity Factor), and how their behavior impacts on all Five Constituencies. Doing so will make your own job as a manager so much easier.

Influence Techniques

Influence is different from power: perhaps you have never looked at it that way? But this is important. Influence is generally viewed as weaker than power and less reliable: there is no guarantee that an influence attempt will work whereas bringing power to bear on a matter or person has a higher chance of getting the desired result – albeit compliance devoid of buy-in and helpful attitude.

Influence is more tactical. This is why I firmly believe business and management schools must teach organizational politics. Instead, the entire business world is chanting the "work is no place for politics" mantra. Adopting such an approach simply sees you dis-empower yourself and surrender control to those who use politics.

But influence is excellent in that it calls for more face-to-face interactions with people. It is amazing what you can get people to do when you're standing right there with them. Children do it to their parents every day! And what power do children have? None: it's all influence on their part – influence and behavior.

How you dress, whether you smile or not, how professional you look, how good looking you are, how tall you are, how well liked you are: these have all been found to have an impact on your ability to influence those around you. Remember this when thinking about yourself and when observing the people around you. How do you or they dress? How do you or they carry yourselves? Are you liked, or respected, or both? Are you sure about that?

You can influence using logical arguments, by using facts, by blinding them with science. You can appeal to a person's goals, their ambitions. You can offer praise, flattery, veiled threats, the possibility of future pain or exclusion or of looking bad in the eyes of others. You can appeal to their friendship with you, a family connection, past favors, rules and policies, precedence, and the weight of other people going in the same direction. You can use budget expectations, resources – the allocation of most things – when trying to influence and persuade people.

So much of what a manager does is based in his ability to influence those around him. If only power was used, people would tire of the manager very quickly and the organization would fail to ever come close to achieving its full potential.

Behavioral Impact – Rules for Success

Now it's time to take everything we have covered so far and tie it all together. Remember, when managing people it is the *behavior* of those people that will ultimately determine their productivity, their efficiency, and the profits they contribute to the bottom line. That's why businesses continue to fail, or corruption cannot be stamped out, or why people get big bonuses despite making their businesses weaker: the focus is on the incentives and the end result – profit, shareholder value, earnings per share – rather than on the *behavior* of such people: manage the behavior and you'll manage into existence the end result you're looking for. And as we saw in the last chapter, following the 5-Ms of intelligent managerial behavior can bring about positive changes in both motivation and behavior.

Here are some simple rules to keep in mind when seeking to subtly and positively alter the behavior of employees without coming right out and announcing you're going to change the way they do things.

Rule 1: Use Cross-Training or Muscle Confusion.

These are concepts taken from the world of exercise and fitness. Cross-training enables you to avoid plateaus: muscles become use to you using the same techniques over and over. Employees can be the same. Mix it up a little. To get a message across, use several channels, several people, several methods. Change your words. Get others talking for you. Training should also have cross-functional and multi-level elements built in to enhance organizational connectedness and overall understanding.

Rule 2: Alternate between Teaching and Questioning.

This keeps people on their toes. It stops you from becoming a domineering know-it-all, and ensures that *you* don't stop listening to the people around you. Remember; power can cause you to start talking more and listening less – not a good development!

Rule 3: Raise their Curiosity.

Instead, for example, of telling a manager that the place is being run in a bad way, ask something like, "I wonder why our competitor across the street doesn't have these problems. It's been bugging me for a while and I can't figure it out. What do you think? How do *they* get employees to greet customers properly and keep the place clean and tidy?" Or, you can be a little more direct: "Can I show you a better way of counting the inventory?" People generally find it hard to resist a little curiosity, so use it. Telling them out straight might create the behavior of resisting. Instead, raise a little curiosity on their part and you might be able to alter such a behavior (the behavior of resisting) or even prevent it from surfacing in the first place.

Rule 4: Make Suggestions Instead of Giving Orders.

Suggesting is telling but in a less direct way. Obviously this is Context Sensitive: there are times when circumstances call for you to tell it as it is and get things done.

Rule 5: Ask.

Asking gets people to think for themselves. It enables you to develop their confidence, their thinking, and reshape their attitude. It can spark their creativity. Every once in a while, *you* might actually learn something too! You never have all the answers – not even close to it! Asking opens so many doors to possibility.

Rule 6: Let Them Think it's all their Own Idea.

Guiding people by raising their curiosity, asking, and then letting them think it out enables you to let them think the solution is all their own. This helps to combat resistance since any later changes are built upon the foundations of their own ideas.

Rule 7: Give Them a Tag to Live up to.

I'll usually say something like, "...and if you want her to see you as being a really good manager you should take ten minutes to chat with her privately..." It's the "being a really good manager" part that acts as an invitation to the person I'm talking to. In simple terms: it's for them to reject the tag and thereby surrender the right to complain. If they refuse to help themselves – live up to the tag I offered them – and things don't improve, blame migrates to *them* and not to me or the employee.

Rule 8: Use Availability Heuristics.

Continually talking about the same thing can create the false impression that it is more widespread than it actually is which in turn can raise its level of importance and peoples' emotional reactions to that thing. Trade Unions will use this approach to get workers to fight against an employer. Pointing to a woman and saying she did her MBA at Harvard and is a billionaire can create the impression that if we all go to Harvard we'll all become billionaires. Get several people saying the same thing using the same example and it soon becomes "truth" or accepted conventional wisdom. The actual truth may simply be that this was an exceptional woman who just happened to have an MBA from Harvard. Indeed, she may have gone to Harvard *after* striking it rich! We saw this idea earlier in the Create Convention Wisdom section in chapter 4.

Rule 9: Use Their Imagination.

Research has shown that my asking you if a particular outcome is possible versus getting you to imagine the outcome first *and then* asking you whether or not it's possible can lead to two different results. Getting you to imagine an outcome first raises your perception of its possibility. Get an employee to imagine a desired end result *before* asking them if they think they can help you and the organization to bring it about. Doing so raises your chances of success.

Rule 10: Work the Boards – Get *Them* Doing it Too!

Ultimately, the aim here is to get everyone working the boards to enhance focus and creativity. Exposure to this technique – when led by a person willing to develop those around him – should lead to everyone using it.

Rule 11: Interact.

Interacting with people alters their behavior. That's because it alters their thinking, their reactions, their perspective and perception. There is no guarantee that the initial reactions will be positive, but there *will* be a change.

Rule 12: Attack in Threes.

This refers back to our earlier point about structuring your conversation. If you want an employee to feel confident, try saying something like: "...that way you'll be safe, assured of success, and know you can make the figures". The human brain has trouble processing more than three presuppositions at a time, so don't over-do it. Don't give them a laundry list of feel-good outcomes. Stick to your three best instead.[84] We see this in the world of sales with the "Feel, Felt, Found" technique. For example, an experienced salesperson will respond to resistance with, "I understand how you [feel]. Many of my clients have [felt] the very same way but when they looked at our approach they [found]..." Not only is this attacking in threes: it introduces empathy, social proof, new discovery, and more.

---

[84] Doing so brings about what Hogan et al (2006) refer to as "Controlled Overwhelm". See p. 100 of Hogan et al.

Rule 13: Become Interested in the Work Issues the Employees are Interested in.

Empower yourself by doing a little digging, listen to what's being said, and prepare to ensure you know your stuff on each issue. This is *not* about becoming a master of the irrelevant.

Rule 14: Be Sincere, Respectful, and Polite.

This does not mean become a doormat or a wimp. When praising or giving a compliment, mean it: be sincere. If you don't mean it, don't say it: people can see through nonsense. Have a little respect. You should never push a person to the point where they break down and burst into tears. You're not out to destroy anyone or attack the person of the employee. And be polite. It doesn't hurt and doesn't take any extra effort. Thank people when they do something. Apologize when you're wrong, on edge, snappy, or do so upfront so they'll understand why you're not quite yourself.

Rule 15: Use Words and Metaphors from *Their* World: Speak *Their* Language.

This enables understanding, clearer vision of what is being discussed. It brings about comfort through familiarity of association, especially when those associations are positive. Use the right metaphors, know what you're talking about, and be sincere and genuine.

Rule 16: Use your Language in an Intelligent Way.

Frame things properly. Prepare. Think it out before you open your mouth. Use "As you know" to get a person onside, to prevent them becoming defensive, to avoid seeming like you're telling them how it is, and to enable them save face if they have a shortfall in knowledge and experience on the subject. This little trick also sets them up subtly to accept new information or points of view. It's a neat little framing trick on your part when used properly. If you feel a person might reject something out of hand, try working an "As you know" into your lead up to the potentially confrontational point.

Rule 17: Move Away from Using "But" or "However" and Toward Using "And".

Remember, people generally forget what came before the "but" because they're becoming defensive and preparing to react to what comes after it. Diffuse this type of behavior by reframing your sentence such that "and" gets used instead: "You explained the system well <u>but</u> you then went on to tell them too much…", versus, "You explained the system well <u>and</u> I think if you stop at that point you'll ensure…" – a subtle difference, but a big effect.

Rule 18: Use the Contrast Effect.

Ask for something a little too big. Then, after the person refuses, ask for what you really want. Your request now seems more reasonable *in contrast* to what you were first seeking: your previous request anchors their mind in the world of "big things" thereby making your request look small.

Rule 19: Identify a Common Enemy.

Focus on a competitor, on costs, on efficiency, on rules and procedures, on slow processes – anything. Doing so gives people a cause to get behind. It's so much better than focusing on why the accounts department is making life difficult for the marketing department and other such feud-filled framings. Then align yourself on their side against this new "enemy" and set goals to defeat it.

Rule 20: Give a Little.

Remember, the trick is to give something that doesn't cost you much but which the other side views as valuable. Give a little time. Listen. Take notes of the suggestions or complaints. Then give them feedback at a later meeting or encounter.

Rule 21: Catch Them Doing Something Right.

By doing this you at least identify a behavior worth reinforcing in an employee. The opposite and more common approach of jumping on someone just as soon as they make a mistake usually only communicates a "don't get it wrong again" message without identifying any specific correct behavior to follow. Refer back to our earlier discussion on finding the Successful Deviant.

Rule 22: Less Training, More Development.

Beyond a certain point, training starts to deliver diminishing returns. Often you will find people very good at working the system but totally incapable of standing up and giving a presentation or taking criticism or being prepared to tackle another person. In simple terms, development is sorely lacking thereby limiting the potential of the individuals and, in time, the entire organization.

Rule 23: Mix Memory Reconstruction with Pygmalion and Self-fulfilling Prophecy.

The human memory is highly *un*reliable and tends to *reconstruct* more than recall. Pygmalion was all about people picking up on signals from their teacher that they were good students or followers, and self-fulfilling prophecy was about bringing about what you believe should come about. Now, so long as a person does not say out loud what they think going into a challenge or exercise, you can alter their memory afterwards. By telling a person they did really well in a challenge, you can cause them to remember – reconstruct – it in a more positive way. In other words, you can boost a person's confidence by getting them to believe after an event that they must have been more confident about it all along. This sets them up well for repeating the challenge or a similar one thereby activating the self-fulfilling prophecy aspect.

Rule 24: Don't be Environmentally Naïve.

This has nothing to do with going green, nature, or plants. We saw earlier how surroundings can have a huge yet subtle impact on behavior. But there's nothing to say you cannot use this incompetence in others to your advantage. Taking a junior manager out to a hugely expensive restaurant or a sales person into an overly lavish boardroom can tilt things in your favor: the environment you select can serve to knock them slightly off balance or create a desired impression.[85] Sit them by a window in the hot sun, or turn the air conditioning up or down, or leave a competitor's business card sticking out of a file – whatever: alter the environment to suit your purposes.

Rule 25: Experiment.

No one approach will work on all people. You'll have to come at them on several fronts, mix it up, change the order, and more. Remember, there is no one-fits-all rule or method of managing. Everything is context sensitive – something you monitor through Constantly Reassess, observation, and experimentation.

Persuading and influencing people – whether covertly or overtly – to do anything *does* lead to behavioral change, albeit in small amounts. But these small amounts have a cumulative effect and benefit over time. You know instinctively that this is true – especially in the opposite direction: allow a child or an employee to get away with more and more little things and soon they'll be out of control. Give people an inch and they *will* take a mile! And you know it works in the positive too, so manage it all to the benefit of the organization.

---

[85] This provides a fascinating potential "rule breaker" to the being humble rule touted by so many gurus at the start of the 21st century, i.e. that you should not have a large and lavish office – that you must be "one of them". Personally, I believe it's always nice to keep a little environment impression management in your arsenal.

Some Final Thoughts

Power comes in many forms and often without rank or title to announce it. It is used in many ways everyday and your ability or inability to accept, recognize, and manage this greatly determines the level of effectiveness you will attain as a manager.

Will simply telling people what to do – using your power – get things done everyday? Most of the time – yes! But there's a subtle and crucial difference between "compliance" and "commitment". Keep using your power and you're headed for compliance: a short-term solution devoid of long-term focus. In so many ways, the use of power is vulgar management: too simplistic. It takes real skill to master influence and the fantastic human benefit – commitment – that can result.

You must recognize that you will get little done alone. This is why power alone is insufficient. It is in the fine mix of power *plus* influence that true effectiveness is to be found.

Conclusion

Lessons for Life

Leading and managing people is about…well…leading and managing *people*! It's not about reports or personnel files that talk about people in distant and abstract terms. Leading and managing people means understanding them; interaction brings understanding. And what does Business & Management School teach you next to nothing about? *PEOPLE*!

Remember; most of what we have covered here applies whether you hold a position within the organizational managerial ranks or not. These are lessons for life – lessons you can apply for all time throughout your career. Indeed, there is ample scope to suggest that not being in the ranks just yet will benefit you since you can spend time in meetings watching to see if you can spot where people are being ineffective and getting in their own way. As I say to people quite regularly, you will often be shocked at the level of ineffectiveness within the managerial and employee ranks. After reading all we have covered thus far, it will not take you long at all to identify the people causing the problems!

If your own manager seems to be ineffective, you can subtly lead in an upward direction by merely Bookmarking the Conversations in your own mind and returning to the main point of focus. Ineffective people will go off on tangents or become too personal or emotional or be easily distracted; you can bring everything to a better conclusion without seeming to takeover: "Yes, I can see what you mean but, I thought the point we were trying to deal with was..." – that right there is what you are after; you Bookmarked the Conversation, brought everyone back to the point, and did it subtly in the form of a non-aggressive question – leading from the bottom is not at all difficult.

A Good Start, a Good Approach

Your starting point should always be to manage *yourself*: it's what most managers overlook and what most business schools never think of! (Go back to *If You Cannot Manage Yourself, You Cannot Manage Others*). You have a Leadership Brand whether you accept this or not; make sure it's a good and consistent one. Then move to your senior team. It is absolutely essential they understand that their loyalty is to this team and *not* to their individual divisions, departments, or silos: get it wrong with your senior team and you can only ever be captain on a ship of fools.

Then, when your senior team is in good shape with the right people in the right places doing the right things, move out to the general body of workers or employees. Leadership and management are *not* about talking to *every* person *all* the time: you are expected to apply what you learn in an intelligent way rather than abandoning all common sense for newly discovered methods. But talking and listening – interacting – are of crucial importance. You need to keep your finger on the pulse. You need to make sure the reports you get are accurate. You need to know when people have been bullshitting you! You need to follow before you lead – embed yourself with the troops for a while; start working for *them* to make sure all is as it seems and should be. Engaging by walking around should be *mental* exercise, not physical.

Spotting Desired Behaviors

Whether it is the directors, the executives, the managers, general employees – whomever – your entire focus must be on behavior: seeing it, understanding what is causing it, managing it. A failure to fully come to terms with this topic can only see you managing the wrong things in the wrong people in the wrong way. Behavior is the main byproduct of conditioning – whether it's children, pets, or workers. The behavior of your executives, managers, and employees is largely the result of conditioning via your managerial philosophy, organizational culture, example setting. *Your* Behavior - accepted norms – conditions *them* to behave in particular ways: Blame (or praise) therefore migrates back to you for the final result.

Our focus here on behavior is not about changing people or altering who they are; you can, for example, get happy or sad or angry or bitter people to answer the telephones on the second ring (the desired behavior) without changing their personalities or anything far-fetched like that.

Remember the three key steps: (1) set the example; (2) incentivize/reward mimicking the suitable example; (3) install metrics to lock the behavior into place.

As you walk around, seek out the Successful Deviants: these are your champions of tomorrow. Take their behavior and what they do and get them to teach it to those lagging behind. If they can't teach, map it and share the knowledge to improve the business as a whole. Remember, the simple step of interacting with people creates a new norm – over time this can impact upon organizational culture. It also affords learning and development opportunities for them *and* for you.

The Crucial Portfolio of Talents

At the start of this book I referenced findings by Gallup indicating that only 10% of managers possessed the talents necessary to enable them come to be viewed as 'great' managers.[86] Those traits, according to Gallup research, are as follows:

- An ability to motivate every single employee with a compelling mission and vision;
- An assertiveness to drive key outcomes;
- An ability to create a culture of clear accountability;
- They build relationships based on trust, open dialogue, and full transparency (let me know if any of this is starting to sound familiar!!);
- An ability to make decisions that are *not* based on politics.

Gallup found that such managers – the rare 10% with these specific talents – actually contribute 48% higher profit to their companies when compared with average managers. Interesting, wouldn't you say?!

Form Your Own Opinions

Steer clear of personnel files until you have afforded yourself the opportunity to see things first hand. Personnel files can very often set you marching in the wrong direction. For example, a lot of "trouble makers" very often are nothing of the sort: their managers might be the problem. Observe, experiment, measure. Try not to rush out to manage people you do not fully understand; to lead, you must first follow. Remember:

---

[86] *Why Good Managers are So Rare*: Randall Beck and James Harter; March 13, 2014. HBR Blog Network.

- Laziness *never* pays, it *always* costs;
- Conventional wisdom is not *necessarily* truth;
- Always start with You!
- Management is so much easier when you don't get in your own way: Choices-Demands-Constraints.

The Power of Words

In the world of management words are powerful – perhaps this has never occurred to you before? A failure to get to grips with words and their potential impact leaves you at the mercy of resulting emotions. Understand words and the meanings people ascribe to them and actions that previously seemed irrational reveal a method to their madness – you can also steer people more effectively through the intelligent use of words and word-meanings.

One of the most powerful words in the business and management vocabulary is "Ask". This little word:

- Is an excellent time management technique;
- Gives you access to knowledge and fast learning;
- Enables you steer your boss without seeming to openly criticize him;
- Enables you to develop people by steering them without overtly telling them what to do;
- Enables you to spark thinking and creativity in the people around you and enables you avoid spoon-feeding the answers to them and bringing about learned helplessness.

Don't Get Sidetracked

There are now two dangerous mindsets rampaging through the business & management world that you need to be very mindful of:

1. "Leader"; and
2. "Specialist".

Simply focus on interacting with people, listening and observing, and getting things done in better ways: Constantly Reassess and become Context Intelligent. Do those things and, over time, the leadership label will come to you. Rather than the title of 'Leader' – thereby suggesting a different form of human being – focus instead on the verb lead*ing*; the 'ing' is the behavior part.

And don't stray so far to the "Specialist" end of the spectrum that you render yourself useless in the majority of daily scenarios and incapable of seeing and understanding the overarching links between concepts and disciplines.

Three Important Groups

To maintain a meaningful and more rounded sense of momentum, shuffle the deck every once in a while: rotate advisors in and out of your in-house network as and when dictated by context and your own progress - using the same people all the time can only get you the same insights and results.

Second, keep an external group loyal to you, not the organization. This will help you reach the best decisions free from in-house politicking and tainted agendas.

Third, keep a group of easy-going pals you can escape to in order to retain your sanity and perspective on life in general. In the end, a job is just a job!

Start Managing, Teaching, Developing

Business & Management schools don't teach you how to manage people and this is compounded by the fact that conventional business wisdom is often common folly. Never lose sight – for yourself and when hiring others – of the things business schools *don't* tell you:

- As a manager, you must teach and develop your employees – training, over time, delivers diminishing returns;
- People are *always* motivated;
- People are *always* creative;
- People are *always* watching and listening and thinking and talking to somebody;
- When dealing with people – especially executives and managers – never assume maturity develops at the same pace a person ages;
- Strive for "Good Enough" and then hit the road adapting as you go: perfection is a journey, *not* a place from which to start.

Leading and managing people should be a two-way street: Collaboration and Mutual Interdependence is your goal with communication as your enabler. Employees must play an active role in being managed. When you use effective listening, they become better talkers. Always aim to use upfront effective listening: sniff out problems before they take root.

Speaking *their* language enables you to be much more effective as a manager: listening to employees also enables you get out of their way. But listening should never equate to wasting your time, to wandering around aimlessly and avoiding your obligations. You are out walking around to keep your finger on the pulse, to make sure the reports you read are accurate, to see what is causing the numbers to add up the way they do in all the reports. Go listen, interpret what you hear, then make a decision on any actions to be taken.

Everything you are doing when interacting with employees has the potential to have a positive impact on – and may even change – your organizational culture. Chatting, asking questions, listening, pushing back on suggestions, testing answers – all these things help to develop people as you lead, manage, and engage by walking around; this is you working for *them*. And all this can be done without launching a large official change program that generates large-scale resistance. Don't get caught up in all this overly friendly hug-your-workers stuff that's going around. That's not what effective management and people development is about.

Remember, if in doubt – call them out! Doing so saves time, surfaces conflict, and enhances your overall ability to manage any given situation. Again, it comes back to communication – the topic upon which everything stands or falls. If you suspect something is not being said, or done, or met - call them out!

You must learn to manage in *all* directions. You can manage your colleagues and those above you in the organizational structure – it's not just about managing those below you. You manage up (communications and expectations, for example) and down the chain-of-command and around all Five Constituencies. But you must also learn to listen in all directions, observe in all directions, and be fully aware that the examples you set travel in all directions: be an intelligent and well-rounded manager.

When you stand back and look at the organization or business, you must be aware that bureaucracy is not bad *per se*. It is your job to determine whether you have too much or too little: is it "Inhibiting" or "Enabling"?

It is also essential you test the *quality* of communication throughout the organization or business. Everything stands or falls on communication issues. It is not enough to know the full range in the human communications repertoire: you must also understand and *manage* this in yourself and in the people around you to reach your full potential as a manager. Always bear in mind that the consequences of a failure on this front are not always readily observable. Many indicators – such as customer dissatisfaction – are lagging in nature: by the time you realize you have a problem, you're dead!

Teaching employees may seem like a pain but it's an up-front effort that ultimately makes your own life easier over the medium to long-term. Remember, one of your ultimate goals is to enable yourself manage people *less* and people manage themselves more. To this end, you must teach the people working with you to question, to Constantly Reassess, to experiment intelligently on a small scale, to read and understand the numbers of the business. If they can do all these things, *you* don't have to – or at the very least, you gain helpers with the ability to improve things.

Always insist on training having cross-functional and multi-level elements designed into the program. Use Error-Based teaching methods, immerse the trainees fully in their training for an extended period of time, leverage the methods used by Positive Deviants in the business, and use portfolio and job rotation to train and develop.

In terms of People Development, you need to get people to the point where they have little difficulty talking openly and positively about their own mistakes and failures. This shows they have ego-strength: an essential ingredient for the truly effective managers of tomorrow. All of your interactions, mutual collaboration, and interdependence help to build their ego-strength.

Diversity is not just about gender and skin color. You are looking for people from different industries, countries, with different experiences – and more. The closer the inside of your company comes to representing the world outside to which it sells, the better.

Delegation is essential for any truly effective manager. It enables you manage your own time, develop employees, and aid in your succession planning. There are four key pillars to effective Delegation:

- *What* to delegate;
- *When* to delegate;
- *How* to delegate;
- *To Whom* delegation should be made.

Then it's simply a matter of behavior on *your* part as you delegate. That behavior is best channeled through the use of the 5-R system:

1. Repeat;
2. Remind;
3. Reinforce;
4. Record;
5. Return.

The Desired End Result

When you get all the people in the organization talking openly, listening in an effective way, defending their ideas and not themselves, moving toward solution-oriented mindsets, sharing insights, working the boards, bookmarking conversations, and accepting delegated tasks, you achieve all of the following:

- You help build their ego-strength;
- You kill off defensiveness in the people around you;

221

- You help them build emotional stability;
- You develop their interpersonal skills;
- You move them from external to internal locus of control;
- You move them toward becoming Context Intelligent;
- You teach them to Constantly Reassess;
- You set and perpetuate suitable example setting;
- You move them from co-acting to inter-acting thereby killing off negative synergies and creating new positive ones.

In simple terms: the results you achieve enable you tackle and prevent all the reasons research over the years states managers derail. By working for them, you are developing people into effective operators, managers – you are teaching them how to lead in given situations irrespective of rank or lack thereof. You are ensuring diversity on the ground, but not diversity of mind: everything we have covered here helps you surround yourself with similar-minded people – people from diverse backgrounds with diverse experience but with similarly high levels of focus, motivation, and energy.

Remember: (1) set or live the example you wish to see in the organization; (2) incentivize/reward mimicking the suitable example; (3) install metrics to motivate, track, and to lock the behavior into place. For continued study of the topics discussed in the *Just Manage It!* series, please visit: www.JustManageIt.com

About the Author

Colm McCormack was born in Ireland, where he spent the first thirty-five years of his life. He is a graduate in business, law, and management from Griffith College Dublin/Nottingham Trent University, and Trinity College, Dublin.

Over the years, in addition to extensive experience in the legal and insurance industries, he has lectured to MBA students and mentored and coached experienced managers and company founders in Ireland and the United States across a wide range of industries.

Colm lives in Virginia, in the United States.

For further information and FREE Article Downloads, visit: www.JustManageIt.com

Bibliography

Armstrong, Michael. (2004) *How To Be An Even Better Manager – A Complete A – Z of Proven Techniques & Essential Skills*. Sixth Edition. Kogan Page.

Blanchard, Ken and Johnson, Spencer. (2004). *The One Minute Manager – Increase Productivity, Profits and Your Own Prosperity*. HarperCollins Publishers.

Carayol, R. and Firth, D. (2001). *Corporate Voodoo – Principles For Business Mavericks And Magicians*. Capstone Publishing Ltd.

Carnegie, Dale. (1998) *Dale Carnegie's Lifetime Plan For Success: The Great Bestselling Works Complete in One Volume*. Galahad Books.

Finkelstein, Sydney. (2003). *Why Smart Executives Fail – And How You Can Learn From Their Mistakes*. Portfolio.

Glasser, William, M.D. (1999). *Choice Theory: A New Psychology of Personal Freedom*. Harper Perennial.

Greenberger, D. and Padesky, C. (1995). *Mind Over Mood: Change How You Feel by Changing the Way You Think*. The Guilford Press.

Grossman, Dave, Lt. Col. (1995). *On Killing: The Psychological Cost of Learning to Kill in War and Society.* Back Bay Books/Little, Brown and Company. New York.

Hamel, Gary (with Bill Breen). (2007). *The Future of Management.* Harvard Business School Press.

Hogan, Kevin, and Speakman, James. (2006). *Covert Persuasion: Psychological Tactics and Tricks to Win the Game.* John Wiley & Sons Inc., New Jersey

Jennings, Jason and Haughton, Laurence. (2000, 2002). *It's Not the Big that eat the Small...it's the Fast that eat the Slow – How to Use Speed as a Competitive Tool in Business.* Harpercollins Publishers Inc.

Jennings, Jason. (2002). *Less Is More – How Great Companies Use Productivity as a Competitive Tool in Business.* Portfolio.

Kim, W. Chan, and Mauborgne, Renée. (2005). *Blue Ocean Strategy: How to Create Uncontested Market Space and Make the Competition Irrelevant.* Harvard Business School Press.

Kingston, William. (2003). *Innovation: The Creative Impulse in Human Progress.* The Leonard R. Sugerman Press Inc.

Kiyosaki, Robert T. (2008). *Rich Dad's Plan For Financial Success: The First Three Bestsellers.* Business Plus.

Loftus, E. (1979) *Eye Witness Testimony.* Harvard University Press.

Manzoni, Jean-Francois, Barsoux, Jean-Louis. (2002). *The Set-Up-To-Fail Syndrome – How Good Managers Cause Great People To Fail.* Harvard Business School Publishing Corporation.

Maxwell, John C. (2004). *Winning with People – Discover the People Principles That Work for you Every Time.* Thomas Nelson Inc. McCormack, Colm. (2008). *Just Manage It! If You Cannot Manage Yourself You Cannot Manage Others.* Create Space Publishing.

Mintzberg, Henry. (2004). *Managers Not MBAs – A Hard Look at the Soft Practice of Managing and Management Development.* Pearson Education Limited.

Patterson, Kerry. Grenny, Joseph. Maxfield, David. McMillan, Ron. Switzler, Al. (2008). *Influencer: The Power to Change Anything.* McGraw-Hill Books.

Patterson, Kerry. Grenny, Joseph. Maxfield, David. McMillan, Ron. Switzler, Al. (2005). *Crucial Confrontations: Tools for Resolving Broken Promises, Violated Expectations, and Bad Behavior.* McGraw-Hill Books.

Pfeffer, Jeffrey. (2007). *What Were They Thinking? Unconventional Wisdom About Management.* Harvard Business School Press.

Pierce, V. (2003). *Quick Thinking On Your Feet.* Mercier Press. Ireland.

Porter, Michael E. (1980). *Competitive Strategy: Creating and Sustaining Superior Performance.* First Free Press/Simon & Schuster, Inc.

Rosenthal, Robert: *Covert Communication in Laboratories, Classrooms, and the Truly Real World*. Current Directions in Psychological Science, 12, 2003, 151-154.

Scaturo, D. J. (2005). *Clinical Dilemmas in Psychotherapy: A Transtheoretical Approach to Psychotherapy Integration*. American Psychological Association.
Schiffman, S. (2007). *Cold Calling Techniques: That Really Work*. Adams Media: Massachusetts.

Teyber, E. (2006). *Interpersonal Process in Therapy: An Integrative Model*. Thomson, Brooks. USA.

Trump, Donald. Zanker, Bill. (2007). *Think Big and Kick Ass In Business and Life*. HarperCollins Books.

Vecchio, Robert P. (2006). *Organizational Behaviour – Core Concepts*. International Student Edition. 6th Edition. Thomson South-Western.

Wachtel, Paul L. (1993). *Therapeutic Communication: Knowing What to Say When*. The Guildford Press. New York.

Wagner, Rodd, and Harter, James. K. (2006). *12: The Elements of Great Managing*. (2006) Gallup Press. New York

Watkins, M. (2003). *The First 90 Days: Critical Success Strategies for New Leaders at all Levels*. Harvard Business School Publishing. Massachusetts.

Just Manage It!
The 'YOU' Factor:
If You Cannot Manage
Yourself
You Cannot Manage Others

"Companies need to rethink how they manage – the 'Just Manage It!' series is taking us there: a new approach, a different script, a better result."
– New York Times Bestselling Author, Jason Jennings

The first book in the "Just Manage It!" series begins where all management books *should* begin – with <u>You</u>, the person. Moving from self-awareness to observation of others and on to a critical look at so much of the business world's conventional and misplaced wisdom, this book is packed with dynamic new models and frameworks, groundbreaking concepts, and insightful wisdom.

The book reaches back beyond the starting point of most other business & management books and into topics most business & management schools overlook. If you want to lead and manage effectively, first learn to manage yourself.

Some of the key topics touched upon include:

- Creating Context Intelligent Managers;
- The Power of Social Contagion;
- The Co-Activity Syndrome;
- Warping the Psychological Contract;
- Listening Fitness;
- The Ten-Ps of Constituency and Context Awareness;
- The Importance of Politics, Ego, and Confrontation.